The Quest

Heal Your Life, Change Your Destiny

Give a Gift that Makes a Difference...

My prayer is that this book reach everyone
it is meant for and that hundreds of millions of people
throughout the planet use TheQuest to heal and
transform their lives so Peace can be restored on Earth

Please Support the Institute of Advanced Healing's Global Outreach Program

Your Tax Deductible donations gift TheQuest books to prisons, rehab centers, hospitals, hospice, safe houses, youth at risk, abuse, anger management, and addiction programs, or the designation of your choice in your name.

Donate & Find out more at:
http://www.AuroraJulianaAriel.com,
http://www.IOAH.org, or http://www.TheQuest.us

Thank you for helping me bring TheQuest to the world.

Aurora Juliana Ariel

Praise for TheQuest

Jack Canfield, author of 'Success Principles' and co-author of the 'Chicken Soup for the Soul' Series: TheQuest session with Aurora was a magical and helpful experience. It unblocked a subtle but powerful limitation in my life. I am grateful to her for her work and for her safe and gentle way of being.

Jared Rosen, Co-Author of 'The Flip' and, 'Inner Security And Infinite Wealth': TheQuest is a ratified healing system that works at such a core level, that ancient subconscious patterns clear at lightning speed. Aurora is truly a master!

Randolph Craft, founder, Pacific Planning Institute, and Pacific International Aging Center: The space Aurora holds for healing is so powerful that one has no choice but to move forward in her Presence.

Aeoliah, Author, Artist, Composer, Recording Artist: I was pleasantly surprised to find Aurora's TheQuest work to be so simple and straightforward, yet at the same time so dynamic and powerful in helping to shift deep-seated limiting energy patterns hidden within my subconscious. I found it to be a most healing experience to give a voice to my deeper feelings and express how I really felt about certain things in my life in a supportive, caring and non-judgmental setting that helped me to transform those patterns into the fulfillment that I desire. During the session I also enjoyed and appreciated the balance between voicing and openly expressing my feelings, and then later tuning into my Higher Self to allow and receive the messages from my own God Presence which made the experience my own personal empowerment that I cherish in my heart forever.

A Physical Therapist and former Christian Evangelist in California: The diminishment of the human condition is based on lack of self worth and esteem, and no amount of verbal affirmation will transform us. It has to come from an Alchemy within. In TheQuest sessions, the very molecules are rearranged, as cells not nourished are now nourished from within. We are truly cleansed from this inner work. This is like a soul clean up, or 50,000 mile check up for the inner being. The best part is that the changes are permanent. I can't believe how changed I am. People notice a calm and clarity. I have not reverted to the pattern since our last session. I cannot think of a better birthday gift than a chance to heal the inner soul of the grief and debris from our years before. —D.J. Martinovich, Physical Therapist, Palm Springs, California

Christopher Connolly, Composer, Recording Artist: Dr. Aurora Juliana Ariel's abilities as a Healer are so remarkable it is hard to put into words. My work with her was so profoundly deeply moving and transformational that I felt as if I had literally been bathed in the serene waters of the Holy Spirit. Her voice and presence guided me to a Divine place of Inner Peace.

A former nurse manager in Wisconsin: TheQuest process is awesome. I have been through a lot of counseling since the age of 18. I knew as an adult child of alcoholics, without a good role model, I was going to need guidance to overcome my past even at that young age. As a nurse, I have also been exposed to mental heath treatment methods in my career. I have never experienced anything as impressive and empowering. Aurora is a wonderful, loving person who creates a safe space for the deepest healing. —*Virginia Furumo, who is now living her dream life in Hawaii*

Michele Gold, Author of 'Angels of the Sea', Artist and Musician: I had been feeling very sad, almost hopeless, which is very unlike my Nature, for quite awhile, and within 24 hours of my TheQuest Counseling session with Aurora, it just lifted. Nothing outwardly changed and yet, I felt happy inside, a peace with where I was at. It was huge. Aurora's healing gifts are very powerful! The energy that had been suppressed inside me came forward and new projects began moving and many new creative ideas were bursting forth. I felt freer than I had felt in many years, happier, and filled with a quiet confidence that was battered for so long, and now was emerging from an ancient cocoon, with new shimmering wings with which to soar. Aurora Juliana Ariel is a rare radiant treasure. Her magnificent alchemical gifts will embrace you and guide you in a manner filled with so much love and compassion, you will feel free, your most profound self validated to emerge and shine. To experience Aurora's powerful healing work is to sit in the center of an exquisite circle of angels, supporting your soul's deepest wish to transform and live the most exceptional, magical life you were born to live.

Kamala Allen, PhD, Author of 'A Woman's Guide to Opening a Man's Heart': Aurora Juliana Ariel channels Mother Mary energy in an atmosphere of unconditional love and profound peace. Her gentle, effective approach to healing is a deep experience of nurturance and transformation.

A Police Officer and High School Teacher in Aspen: Dr. Ariel's method of going inside one's self and healing past issues or gaining self-realizations is really quite amazingly simple, yet very valuable. Almost like finding a key to a hidden treasure. —*Brad Onsgard, Aspen, Colorado*

A teen in Hawaii: TheQuest is a great way to get things off your chest and deal with feelings that have been deep inside and yet are effecting us in a negative way. It really works! —*Aradeus Zachariah Daffin, 16 years old, Maui, Hawaii (Dr. Ariel's youngest son, now 21, received TheQuest Master Counselor Training with Dr. Ariel for 18 months and co-facilitated the first TheQuest Teen Forum with her in Aspen)*

A mother of an angry, violent eight-year-old: My daughter is doing really well! Thank you so much for working with her, I can really tell a difference in her self-esteem and overall well-being. I can see she really feels great about her appointments with you! After two sessions, three teachers called and asked what happened to her, she had changed so much! Namaste. —*Kelly Sundstrum, Carbondale, Colorado*

A mother whose son was traumatized by a fatal accident where he was the driver: Aurora, you are our angel. You accomplished in five days what doctors and other professionals around us believed would take 8 months for my son to fully recover and get to. Being with you this short time, my son is a changed person. I am very grateful! —*Patti S., Colorado Springs, Colorado*

And others....

Aurora's mastery shines as she navigates us through the terrain of our soul, allowing all of our self to be seen and expressed, thus granting greater freedom, wisdom, and insight. With her keenly trained mind, she lovingly and compassionately guides us in and through the closed doors and murky waters of our unexpressed parts, revealing hidden resources that bring solutions to our every day life, catalyzing deep awakening and a greater understanding of our self. —*Rev. Adrianna Levinson, Vibrant Life Center, Maui, Hawaii*

After years of being in and out of therapy I had changed my life very little but after four Counseling sessions with Aurora I was a new person. I had come to the first session a skeptic, but by the time we were done I was totally amazed by the amount of healing that took place. I had been hitting my head against the wall not getting any movement in my years of therapy. Traditional therapy had only scratched the surface, whereas TheQuest dove right into the root of the issue, uncovered the truth, and healed that aspect of my inner self. The sessions have been the most powerful events in my life. I'm finally free of the unhealthy part of myself that was holding me back for years. I never thought transformation like this was truly possible. I'm no longer a victim of the past and my emotional traumas have been set free. I have my life back! I've made more progress in a few sessions with Dr. Ariel than I have in years of therapy. —*Lance Koberlein, Programmer Real Estate Broker Entrepreneur, Denver, Colorado*

I had pronated knees since I was a little girl. Continually aggravating the condition through a very active and full life, it became a life long affliction. By 25 years old I had to stop running, a great passion in my life! I also loved to ski, hike, and bike, but my knees would get so sore that my lifestyle was greatly hindered. At TheQuest Life Mastery Training Course in Aspen, I had the opportunity to work with Dr. Ariel. In my session we traced a pattern back to early childhood where I had suffered severe abuse. As we unlocked and healed the pattern, I felt a tremendous release. The very next day I was working out at the Aspen Club gym when, looking in the mirror, I noticed my legs were straight. My trainer came over and could hardly believe his eyes. The condition was healed!
—*Diane Argenzio, Estate Manager, Aspen, Colorado*

Gone are the days of long drawn out traditional therapies! With Aurora's 'TheQuest' work, I have found a way to heal and transform any pattern or history from ancient to present times. The space she creates in her sessions is nurturing, loving, empowering and safe. I have found a new sense of purpose in life with each healing of the darker aspects of myself, a greater love for all that I am. TheQuest allows me to address issues as they come up and access the core of the issue to transform it all in one session! I am so grateful for Aurora's dedication to the healing arts and her loving presence, which has empowered me as a wife, mother, businesswoman, healer, and human being. —*Colleen Lisowski, Business Owner/Healer, Kula, Hawaii*

Since the session I have a very clear mind, not used to it. All energy is there and the creativity is fully able to explode into any direction it needs to without any interruption. Wow! Still settling in the experience and taking apart the system for a deeper grasp and understanding. —*Arben Kryeziu, Business, Marketing, and Internet Consultant*

I thank the Angels for the day Aurora walked into my life! —*Jason Kitchens, Entrepreneur, Grants Pass, Oregon*

My heart is so open and full from this work. Being gently led through the deepest, darkest places leaves only gratitude, love and freedom. In every session we come quickly to the taproot of the issue, create safety for its exposure and transformation, and watch the magic with awe as the entire tree is healed. This work helps me feel so purposeful; proud to be a human, finally. The tools that Aurora uses for healing are pure magic, like laser surgery for the soul. The operation is fast, relatively painless and totally effective. People would not choose to live with pain if they knew this was available. Miracles with Aurora are commonplace. In every session I have the experience that something very profound has taken place, something life changing of a permanent nature. The power of love to heal used to be an expression. After working with Aurora it is a fact. This gentle, precise soul surgeon is a master at healing. —*Miriam Mara, Business Consultant, Boca Raton, Florida*

I feel differently. My attitude has changed. I definitely have transcended my pattern. I am a whole new being! TheQuest session was like an exorcism, casting a demon out of my being that was like a leach, sucking the life force out of me, and preventing me from being who I am as a person. After one session, I am a completely different person. —*Bruce Travis, Author, Real Estate Broker, Wailea, Hawaii*

After 20 years of being intimately involved in the human potential movement, reading endless material, attending every conference I could, listening to speakers, reading their books, and applying their principles, I was never taken to the places I was told they would take me. They just didn't hold up and I would soon be back into my old patterns without knowing why things were not working for me. Then I met Aurora and started receiving TheQuest sessions. Right away, after the 1st session, I realized there was a deeper place I needed to go to resolve the issues in my life. I learned of the importance of finding the root of the problem instead of adopting a philosophy which doesn't eliminate the effect things have had on my life. My life has changed considerably with the elimination of stress, eliminating guilt and frustration, and knowing I can be completely honest with myself and those around me. My self-esteem has been restored to a new high. Each day I look forward to meeting new people, making friends, creating relationships, and enjoying new, and exciting experiences. There is a new outlook on life that has never been there before, and I am free to achieve my goals and aspirations. I am so grateful for this life changing experience of TheQuest. —*Bill Mollring, Business Owner*

Aurora brings a special presence to her work as higher energies work through her causing transformation for the individual. I have personally experienced this and have benefited by releasing, clearing, and transforming at a very deep level. Experiencing her work has helped me to take my own healing work to a deeper and more powerful level. —*Lisbeth Johnson, Certified Rolfer, Columbus, Ohio*

I went from panic to peace in my session. It was incredible. Through this work, I'm feeling a new sense of well being. Everything is shifting. Sometimes I don't even recognize this new person. I am healing after 57 years in life, finally getting 'it' with the help of my guide, Dr. Ariel. —*Kamalia Vonlixfeld, Owner, Lotus Galleries, Kauai*

The session was incredible! I am so much less fearful. Even though it seems that nothing has changed in the physical, I see things differently. —*Mary Miller, Editor*

My life is very changed. I am showing up differently in my relationship with my husband, my son and others. TheQuest has brought me a renewed sense of faith in the Divine. —*DB. Healer/Mother, Maui, Hawaii*

Aurora embodies the violet flame. Transformation and healing occur in her presence. She is a miracle as is every experience I have with her. Colors are brighter, scents are sweeter, sounds are crisper, air is clearer. Working with Aurora is like buying a shuttle pass to Heaven. The entire experience of being human is a greater joy as a result of these clearings. —*Julie Mara, Business Consultant, Kihei, Hawaii*

I thank Aurora you for her deep and compassionate listening. She has a very special gift and I feel grateful to get to connect and experience it. I was able to be more honest with myself about my feelings and needs in my relationship with a very close friend with a life threatening illness. My opening up with her brought us closer together. TheQuest also enhanced my meditation experience, which was really great. They go together very well. —*Paula Mantel, Owner/Educator/Producer, Discovery Learning Systems, Honolulu, Hawaii*

My work and life has really changed and continuing to change because of working with Dr. Ariel. On top of that I have felt really seen by her which has encouraged me to come out more with who I am in the world, something most others cannot do for me since they are not where I am, and don't understand. Her style of counseling resonates with me because it feels very organic to me, creative and natural in working with the psyche and what wants to be seen, acknowledged, transformed, and that our beings want this and know how to do it with help and encouragement and love. This has been an incredible door for me, and my clients are really benefiting. It is helping me to become who I am and what I am here to do. I'm feeling rather teary now with gratitude for divine guidance in meeting Dr. Ariel and the serendipity of life when we open to spirit. —*Lisbeth Walters, Rolpher and Cranial Sacral Practitioner, Columbus, Ohio*

I feel lighter... I loved the process! I have been thinking so much about everything I experienced! Many thoughtful doors have opened and I love the unfolding. It has been helping to shape the way I think and feel about my loves in my life and the lesson they bring. —*Elli Clauson, Special Ed Teacher, Aspen, Colorado*

TheQuest: Heal Your Life, Change Your Destiny

TheQuest is a gift to our planet from the Angelic Realms, which transforms and blesses all who choose to surrender to the Love and Grace of the Soul. Aurora holds the keys to this sacred process, which liberates energies trapped for lifetimes, allowing true Freedom and Peace to become the basis for a happy, fulfilling life. —*Mirra Rose, Spiritual Teacher, International Speaker, Healer, Wailea, Hawaii*

In my class I got to see a side of Aurora that impresses me to no end. Both the spiritual side, but also the vulnerable sharing and compassionate side that has such great love, desire, energy, and compassion to help the world and a great mind to go with all that. She really connected to the kids and I guarantee that is not an easy thing to do these days. She will make a difference and I feel very fortunate I somehow was blessed I got to meet her. My hat's off to her in a big way. —*Brad Onsgard, Aspen High School Teacher and Law Enforcement Officer*

The tools Aurora shared about in her TV interview are so simple, flow easily and have helped me already. I sent an Email about her work to others, and several of us have instantly benefited. The arrangement of her process was much easier than others I've tried. Maybe it is just time for things to be easy. I especially was touched that Aurora allowed the interviewer to be a facilitator, as this shows others that even amateurs can assist healing. I was also impressed that she allowed herself to be the subject. This sends a great message that healers need healing too. I commend her for that openness. —*Libby Coulter, Maui*

When meeting with a court-ordered youth, I noticed an enormous shift in his attitude and responsibility in a very short period of time... So I asked him "What has happened to cause you to mature so quickly?" That's when he told me that he was in a program for teens (TheQuest Teen Forum) that was making a huge difference for him. While he still has a way to go in his life, I have not seen such a huge internal shift in a youth like this in a very long time. My interest in the TheQuest came from seeing results, not from hearing about the program. Fantastic work! —*Shawn Stevenson, MSW, Youth At Risk Counselor, Case Manager for Youth Zone*

AURORA JULIANA ARIEL PHD

The Quest

Heal Your Life
Change Your Destiny

7 Steps to Radically Transform Your Life

A Breakthrough Self Healing System

Aurora Juliana Ariel, PhD
Creator of TheQuest™ and Award Winning Author of the Earth 2012 Series

Books & Music by Dr. Aurora Ariel
#1 Best Selling, Award Winning Author

Earth 2012: The Ultimate Quest - Vol 1
How To Find Peace In a World of Chaos

Earth 2012: Time of the Awakening Soul - Vol 2
How Millions of People Are Changing Our Future

Earth 2012: The Violet Age - Vol 3
A Return to Eden

TheQuest: Heal Your Life, Change Your Destiny
A Breakthrough Self Healing System

Renaissance of Grace
Aurora's World Music CD with Bruce BecVar

Gypsy Soul, Heart of Passion
Gypsy World Music CD by Bruce BecVar & Aurora

River of Gold
New Age Music CD by Bruce BecVar and Aurora

AVAILABLE IN BOOK STORES WORLDWIDE

A New Frontier In Multimedia Arts
Inspired Music, Books, & Films

Publisher: AEOS, Inc.
PO Box 433, Malibu, California 90265
Ph: 310-591-8799   Fax: 413-521-8799
Email: Info@AEOS.ws
Website: http://www.AEOS.ws

Art Direction by Aurora Juliana Ariel
Cover & Interior Design by Aurora Juliana Ariel
Interior Design Master by Kareen Ross
Editing by Aurora Juliana Ariel, PhD
Bio Photos by Monique Feil & Christian Cooper

TheQuest: Heal Your Life, Change Your Destiny
Copyright ©2009 by Aurora Juliana Ariel, PhD.

All Rights Reserved. No part of this book may be used or reproduced in any manner whatsoever without written permission except in the case of brief quotes embodied in critical articles and reviews. For information please address Publisher.

TheQuest™ is a cuting edge Counseling Theory and Practice, comprehensive body of knowledge, and complete Self Healing System with tools to heal an ailing humanity. It is the hope of the publisher that it fulfills its mission in reaching everyone it is meant for across the planet.

TheQuest is a proprietary trademarked Healing System. The publisher and author of this material make no medical claims for its or TheQuest use. This material is not intended to treat, diagnose, advise about, or cure any illness. If you need medical attention, please consult your medical practitioner.

Printed in the USA by Lightening Source

FIRST EDITION
Library of Congress
ISBN 978-0-9816501-6-6

Dedication

TheQuest
is my legacy to my children,
To humanity and to a world in need of healing.
It is a saving grace, a healing salve, and
a miracle in the darkest hours.
May it fulfill its purpose in setting humanity
free to live their Highest Destiny Potential
May all who read these words,
partake of this body of knowledge,
and use TheQuest to restore their lives,
understand that when we heal our lives,
We change our destiny and that of the planet.
It is then Peace can return to Earth.

Acknowledgments

With the deepest Gratitude and Love
I acknowledge and thank…

The many incredible teachers who have shed light on my pathway, too numerous to name.

My beautiful children, Mariah, Araphiel, Gabriel and Aradeus. Your wisdom beyond your years taught me we are ageless beings, your sense of adventure and fun have given me a lifetime of magical experiences, and your preciousness has given me a heart for the children of this world. Thank you for your love and belief in me.

My mother, Dorothy. Your courageous journey speaks to the power of the human spirit to overcome and find value in every challenging circumstance. Your illness inspired my quest to uncover what was at the heart of suffering in our world. If you had not made this descent into what has been one of the darkest experiences a soul could endure, I would never have been catalyzed to search for a cure for suffering or find that in TheQuest. That you have been able to see the 'real me' has been a tremendous support through the years. I thank you with all my heart. Your belief in me has made a great difference in my life.

While I have had many supportive friends, I must especially thank Arya Bruce BecVar for your incredible belief in me and all the love, support, assistance, and true friendship you've given me over the years that has helped me to birth my life's work.

Grandmaster Kimo Pang for sharing your wealth of knowledge with me and entrusting me with the Kahuna Lineage. You gave me the key to the uncharted realms of the psyche, which helped pave the way for my most landmark research and work. Mahalo!

Drs. Ron and Mary Hulnick and the University of Santa Monica (USM), for your exceptional M.A. course in spiritual psychology, which allowed me to master many of the cutting edge counseling practices of the last century and gave me the keys to develop my own Counseling Theory and Healing Practice. Ron, thank you for taking time out of your full life to come onto the faculty to be my Mentor during my doctoral program, and for your extraordinary insights during that crucial time in my life.

Joe Sugarman for your timely support of AEOS so that I could release this body of knowledge to the world. Thank you for your friendship and belief in me.

Tara Grace for your love, support, and belief in me, and your timely support of AEOS, which is assisting me to bring out my life's work.

Marc Ivey, for your sponsorship and support of AEOS that came at the perfect moment in time to help launch my life's work.

Cameron Johnson, for your support and brilliant insight on how I could get TheQuest into the hands of everyone it is meant for.

Kareen Ross for your beautiful interior book design.

Christian Cooper for the great photo shoot.

Shakti Navran, Linda Deslauriers, Shalandra Abbey, and Toby Neal of my writer's group on Maui, for all your insights, enthusiasm, and support while writing this book.

Kaitlyn Keyt and Theresa for showing up royally as true friends at this exciting moment in time as I'm bringing out my life's work.

And my dearest friends, Bernadette and Chester, Melea, and Vajra, who have walked every step of the way with me as I developed TheQuest, wrote this book, and brought out my life's work. Thank you for all your love, support, and belief in me.

Contents

Acknowledgments 17
Introduction 21

Part One: Heal Your Life, Change Your Destiny
   1. A New Horizon 25
   2. An Illumined Pathway 27
   3. Traversing The Inner World 29
   4. Enter the Kahuna 33
   5. Journey Into the Shadowlands 37
   6. Unlocking the Secret Code 39
   7. Rewriting Destiny 43

Part Two: TheQuest
   1. The Secret Formula 49
   2. The Wounds From Your Past Can Be Healed 57
   3. TheQuest Life Mastery Path 67
   4. Self Counseling With TheQuest 71
   5. Creating Time For Your Healing 79
   6. TheQuest Seven Steps 83
   7. The Doctrine of Pain 87

Part Three: TheQuest Seven Master Keys
   1. Take Back Your Power 95
   2. You Are Not Your Patterns 97
   3. Eliminate the Virus In Your Human Computer 99
   4. Walk Your Highest Destiny Path 101
   5. There is No True Victimhood 103
   6. Challenging People Serve You 107
   7. Suffering is Not the Will of God 109

Part Four: The Last Frontier
   1. The Quest For Truth 115
   2. Spiritual Bypass Is Making You Ill 119
   3. Finding Your Soul Purpose 125
   4. Removing the Stains From Your Soul 129

5. Shepherd Your Shadow 133
   6. Healing Your Core Wound. 139
   7. The Final Step: Healing Addictions For The Last Time 145

Part Five: Miracles of TheQuest
   1. Birth of TheQuest 153
   2. Out Of The Darkness Into The Light 157
   3. Redemption 167
   4. TheQuest Session That Saved Three Lives 173
   5. Doorway To A Cure. 177
   6. Fat Crippled Orphan Boy With Glasses 179
   7. More Miracles Of TheQuest. 183

Addendum:
   1. About The Author 191
   2. TheQuest and The Institute of Advanced Healing 193
   3. AEOS 199
   4. Healing Inspired Media 200
   5. Aurora Juliana Ariel's Products 201
   6. Aurora's Books. 202
   7. Aurora's Music. 204

Forward

As so often is the case, Dr. Ariel's personal challenges catalyzed her on the quest that is now changing lives worldwide. Her story speaks to the human spirit who rises from the ashes, overcomes every challenge, seeks to find meaning in each trial, and translates life challenges into an offering for humanity.

She has suffered what many suffer on Earth and come through victoriously, proving a way for people to restore their lives no matter what they've been through. She says, "The pain people carry not only burdens the mind and infects one's perceptual reality, it eventually etches itself upon the physical body, causing illness and aging. Aging is not natural. It is simply the accumulation of life's hard hits. To heal the cause of aging, illness, and other dire conditions, you must heal your deep-seated wounds, fears, pain, and trauma. Otherwise, they will adversely affect your life, limit your passion, creativity, and joy, and cause you to feel old before your time."

Dr. Ariel's search for the cause of suffering and a cure began early on, when her mother became seriously mentally ill when she was 19. Standing by her mother through 23 hospitalizations, she sought remedies to alleviate her mother's suffering, helping her to have a more quality life.

Another powerful catalyst came at 33, when Dr. Ariel had two heart attacks within 6 months, and found she had contracted an incurable heart condition that could debilitate her quickly to death. Willing herself to live, she entered a healing path that led her deep into the psyche to unlock the causes behind her illness. Her landmark discoveries have given her a profound understanding of the psyche, tools to heal an ailing humanity, and a cure she is now gifting the world in TheQuest.

The immense obstacles she faced over many years helped pave a way that is helping lives all over the planet. Through TheQuest Life Mastery Path, people can gain mastery over their psychology, heal their addictions and patterns, and live healthier lives. Through TheQuest Self Healing System, they can emerge from devastating experiences unscathed, with the underlying cause healed.

Upon meeting Aurora, no one would ever imagine what she has been through. Her carefree spirit, youthful appearance, and love for humanity demonstrate the healing power of TheQuest. Like many valiant souls before her, she translated excruciatingly painful experiences into a victorious story and offering for humanity.

It is this commitment and unswerving devotion to a higher purpose that helped her forge a gift for the world out of her own struggle. Her Life is a testimony that every issue can be resolved, every pattern healed, and the conditions of our lives changed. In this way, our healing helps transform the world. Dr. Ariel has paved the way.

Mariah Brown
Daughter of the Author
Maui, Hawaii

Introduction

It was the aftermath of the crash. Everything was spinning around me, a world in shock and despair. The global economic crises had everyone in its grip. I stood at the edge of time, wondering if my destiny was going to be stopped. How could I be birthing my life's work at such a moment?

Major upheavals were taking place in my life. My mother's cancer returned and a host of other dramas crashed upon me. I felt like I was losing my son to drugs and my daughter became deathly ill.

Falling under the weight, I turned to TheQuest, my greatest ally, and was restored. To my amazement, I became a living white fire of determination to bring this healing technology to the world. I knew it was my time, what I had worked on forever. People needed it more than ever and I was on fire to get it to everyone it was meant for. I looked to the Heavens and said, "I am not stopping!"

I have been passionate about my life's work and all the amazing discoveries I've made and at last, TheQuest is helping people around the world. Sharing this body of knowledge in my first book, *Earth 2012: The Ultimate Quest, How To Find Peace in a World of Chaos*, I began to hear from people from different parts of the world who were relieved to find this powerful healing system and apply it in their lives. In the words of one woman in Australia, "I went into the local bookstore and your book made me buy it. When I returned home and delved into the content, I realized why! I need TheQuest!"

This was incredibly heartening, but now the world was being shaken and people around me were devastated. Daily, the news blared impending doom about the ricocheting catastrophe we were in. This was certainly no time to be writing my second book in the Earth 2012 series, but I kept on. I was determined to bring its message of hope to a world in travail. TheQuest kept clearing the way and I continued to feel that fire blazing, compelling me to the finish line.

At one point, I was on a phone conference with Cameron Johnson, a brilliant entrepreneur who created twelve successful businesses from the time he was nine. Now in his early 20's, he had written a book, "You Call the Shots," and had been the runner up in Oprah's 'Big Give.' I had listened to his compelling story at Mark Victor Hansen's 2009 Mega University for Authors.

All the greats were there, sharing their secrets of success. I was especially moved by Cameron's ability to create success out of nothing. Seemed a perfect match, since my main investor had been hit in the crash and key funds were now delayed. The dilemma I shared with this creative marketing genius was, "How can I let people know about my work with no money for marketing?"

Cameron was brilliant as usual. He had reviewed my situation thoroughly and in one flash of genius said, "You need to give away something really valuable, something that can touch people and generate interest in your work." Immediately, TheQuest came to mind. He went on, "You need to give it away for free so that people have something they can treasure and feel the value of." Brilliant I thought!

After the call I sat in wonder. This is how I could fulfill my mission. I was so happy and excited, I could barely sleep that night. I had found a missing piece to my life puzzle. I did not have to wait until I was on Oprah and famous. People could be using TheQuest Tools to heal and transform their lives even before I was known.

I could gift the E-book to the world for FREE forever, but how would I gift the paperback books? They were costly and, where would I find the time to write a complete book? Then an ingenious idea came to mind. I realized I had already written so extensively on the subject, it would be easy to add to it and have the book ready in time to give as a Christmas gift to the world!

So began my triumphant march to create this book, and despite all the personal, local, and global challenges, I not only finished book two in the Earth 2012 series on time for it's June release, but TheQuest book in time for Christmas!

I then remembered the Global Outreach Program I had set up under the Institute of Advanced Healing to bring out TheQuest worldwide. This would be the vehicle to get the books out! Tax Deductible donations would gift the books to the people who need it most at rehab centers, safe houses, prisons, hospitals, youth at risk, addiction, abuse, anger management, and other programs in the sponsor's name. It would be a community by community effort.

Today I am the happiest person in the world, because the trials I've endured in this life have translated into this offering for humanity. The stage is set... A grand mission begun!

Part One

Heal Your Life
Change Your Destiny

CHAPTER ONE

A New Horizon

Over the years, I've continually seen miracles with the TheQuest. So many, that it has compelled me to bring this healing technology to the world. At my darkest hours, it has been my saving grace, allowing me to transcend the most challenging situations and emerge unscathed from the most devastating circumstances.

The many victories in my life are a testimony to the TheQuest and its ability to change sad movies into wondrous learning experiences where you advance and grow tremendously, gain wisdom and insights that are invaluable, and reframe your life to a clear understanding of how your challenges served you. Its ability to release you from suffering is unparalleled in anything I've found on the planet. If there was anything faster that could give this same depth, understanding, learning and growth, I would have incorporated it into the 7 Steps.

In this book, I speak of a lifestyle, a Life Mastery Path that is empowering and life changing. Mastery is the key, and I train you how to gain this self mastery, to stop settling, stop living a limited or dysfunctional existence, and reclaim your authentic power. Not only that, I have a special formula that can help you remove the scars that have stained your life and made you feel unworthy.

These deep seated wounds can be healed and your life transformed. When you gain a greater sense of who you are, you will easily let go of false beliefs and give yourself a better life. No matter how much you have been told you're not good enough, you will finally know that you are powerful, amazing, and rare, someone to love, treasure, and feel good about. You will begin taking great care of yourself, because you will know you are deserving of the best life can offer. Limitations will fall away, and that which once handicapped you will become the fuel to fire your greatest dreams and passions and power you to their fulfillment.

If you have lived with an addiction or situation that has become unbearable, if you've tried to break away, but it has you in its grip, if you feel you can't go on, there is a way out. You don't need to live in pain or be saddled with a life sentence without parole. There is a master solution to your dilemma and a key to set you free, and you will find it in this book.

If you are falling under the weight of immense pressures, feel there is no cure for your unhappy circumstances; if you feel trapped, lost, unmotivated or in the grip of addictions running your life, you are not alone. Many people are suffering in this world and don't know why, but I know and I am going to tell you. Not only that, I am going to give you a cure. If this book does what I hope it will, the silent chord of misery echoing through our world will be lifted. People will emerge from prisons of discontent to live happier, healthier lives. Empowerment will replace martyrdom and self sabotaging patterns will be reprogrammed, resulting in success. A new mastery will be the keynote of our Earth experience, rather than disempowerment, misery, and pain.

Why is suffering such a huge part of your life? Why are your dreams so hard to realize? Through years of pioneering work in the psyche, I delved deeply into these questions and made many landmark discoveries. I found the cause of suffering and how it has passed down through generations of time, until all of us are infected with it. No one emerges into adulthood unscathed.

The good news is that suffering can be healed and quickly. We can feel devastated, depressed, or stressed, and then in minutes we can feel relieved, empowered, and at peace. I've not only proven this way, I live this way. Consequently, the challenges I face are dealt with quickly and effectively. I continually bring my best self to each equation, because I clear the upset, trauma, or pain first. Then I proceed forward, empowered and clear, taking the wisest action steps, and you can do this too.

In countless sessions, I've traced adverse conditions of every kind to subconscious programming and went a step further. I was able to isolate the programs in charge of life challenges and heal them and, I am going to show you how.

In Part One, I take you through my Journey of Healing and how TheQuest was birthed. In Part Two, I lay out the Self Healing System I developed, including TheQuest 7 Step Self Counseling Technique that is fast and easy to apply. In Part Three, I share some amazing secrets in the 7 Master Keys to Inner Peace. In Part 4, I take you into the uncharted realms of the psyche and show you the truth about life's most compelling dilemmas, and in Part 5, you will read about Miracles of TheQuest so landmark, they can inspire your own healing journey and path to success.

CHAPTER TWO

An Illumined Pathway

It feels important to share that I have not come to the conclusions in this book from merely a philosophical standpoint. Nor have I been transported into the amazing peace, joy, and aliveness I experience most of the time merely from applying spiritual principles. While these can help considerably, a greater mastery must be attained if we are going to skillfully traverse our life challenges. There is a powerful part of us that must be excavated if we are going to realize our full potential. If we want to completely heal and transform our lives, we must do some deep inner work.

Like many on earth, I have walked in the trenches, passed through enormously painful experiences, and had immense Mount Everests to climb. Through my own personal quest I found a way to not only alleviate suffering but to cure it. Years of research directly in the psyche allowed me to gain a wealth of knowledge that helped me to change my life from within, and share this Life Mastery Path with others.

As glorious and fulfilling as this journey has been, my life has not been easy. Fraught with challenges of every kind, I was compelled to find a way out of the misery that is so inherent in this world. Through this quest, I made many exciting discoveries and found a way to free myself from the lineage of pain that was traversing my family line.

I have been deeply wounded and like many people, have passed through the most excruciatingly painful experiences. I have suffered great loss and the devastation of my dreams. I have been hated, despised, turned against, dishonored and betrayed.

The only reason I am standing here today with an open heart, a deep sense of peace, and a passion for living is because I found a way to free myself from the subconscious patterns that were causing havoc in my life, and the self sabotage that was continually undoing the good I was striving to create. This resulted in the development of this breakthrough Counseling Theory and Healing Practice.

While I train and certify counselors in TheQuest, one of my greatest joys and what I am the most passionate about, is passing this technology to the layperson as a complete Self Healing System, and then watching it completely change their life.

CHAPTER THREE

Traversing The Inner World

When we take our life experiences to a deeper level, we begin to unlock the mystery of our True Identity. But many of us are scared to venture into the dark regions of the psyche, especially when we are in pain or feel angry, because we are not sure what we will find.

The myths we have been fed since childhood might be true. We may discover that our emotions are just the tip of the iceberg and that we really are bad at our core. We imagine monsters lurking deep within us too horrific to face. It is enough that their voices burst out of us when we least expect it.

We've been ravaged by uncontrolled emotions until we've believed that something is very wrong inside. When we feel out of control, our anger scares us. We look in the mirror and see a hideous contorted face we don't know and don't want to, so we never really know why we are upset. We think we're getting angry over something in the moment, but the truth is, an ancient wound has been awakened in us and the part of us that is wounded is crying out in pain.

We focus instead on who made us angry, who made us feel small, and we blame them. It is so much easier because then we don't need to take responsibility for how we feel. Keeping our attention on what the other person did wrong, insures us that we need never venture inside to find out the truth about ourselves, and our responsibility in the dynamic.

Over time, we've learned to ignore this voice of pain, to push it down, to lock it in the caverns of the psyche and to cover it over with tons of earth so it can't escape and we don't need to feel it.

We've become masters at ignoring our emotions, believing they are bad, and we feel uncomfortable in our skin because we sense something is not right. But what do we do when our emotions become so loud or our depression so strong that we can no longer ignore its voice of pain? When the only way out is within? What if we have to venture down into the dark craggy canyon of our psyche to find the answers? Will we get lost? Will darkness overcome us? Is it a land of no return? Not if you have the right tools.

When you have the courage to go inside and embrace the part of you that is hurt, you unlock a mystery about yourself, your heritage, and your destiny that you could only have found within. Your conscious mind simply doesn't have the capacity to access the deeper truth of what is really going on. It does not remember who you are or where you came from.

There are parts of us that can help us understand our life challenges, once we work with them. They can also help us remember why we are here and what this earthly experience is all about, but they must be uncovered before they can share their truth. When you go within, lost memories surface, and you are reminded of your true heritage and purpose in this life.

Jewels of wisdom beyond price and latent abilities you never dreamed you had inside of you are waiting to be excavated. This is a journey that can lead you to a treasure so vast that it can completely change your life.

We are multifaceted diamonds, but we've become flawed. We have great potential, but we walk through life handicapped, believing we are so much less than we are. The pain from our past has been etched in time. We carry these scars and they permeate our life, coloring our most glorious moments and ruining our most important relationships.

Each time you courageously follow your emotions to the source of your discontent, you find a deep wound and core patterning that is ready to be healed. This pattern has colored your life through its endless dramas, and it will keep repeating the same life lesson for you over and over again until you are ready to listen and do the inner work. Through the deep inquiry TheQuest provides, you can get to the heart of your emotions so you have a clearer understanding of what is going on beneath the surface. When your life passage makes sense, you have greater peace.

Your feelings are the voices that call you to unlock the puzzle of this inner patterning, so it is important that you listen to them. Like drumbeats coursing through you, they draw your attention within.

Following this pathway, you begin to explore what is at the heart of your pain. It is then you have taken the first steps to restoring peace in your Inner World.

Through countless inner treks, I found there is no broken part of us that can't be repaired, no inner monster that can't be healed. There is a way to restore ourselves, and this is how we can return to our innate wholeness. Yes, there are shadowlands to traverse and unhealed wounds to face. There is pain to be released and ruins to be excavated, but beneath it all is something very precious, and a dragon is protecting this lair.

That dragon is a shadow of our True Self that lurks beneath the surface of our conscious awareness, dictating the course of our life. It is the accumulation of our addictions, patterns, and false sense of self, and it must be healed for us to access its treasures. These treasures are lost aspects of ourselves, our lost power, confidence, creative genius, intelligence wisdom, skills, and talents.

If we allow ourselves to be driven by our shadow rather than our higher nature, we will never realize our full potential and our life will be so much less than our dreams. Hardships, challenges, suffering and setbacks will be our lot in life, not the glorious advancement we are capable of.

On my own Inner Quest, conquering each dragon and claiming each treasure became an art. Each time I would emerge awake and clear, wielding a greater portion of my Authentic Power. This is Diamond Work where each flawed or broken facet is repaired until the Diamond Self is completely restored.

CHAPTER FOUR

Enter the Kahuna

Having traversed the most challenging experiences, I could not have made it through unscathed without TheQuest, because everything I went through was so severe. There were times when I could no longer smile. Life had taken its toll. The immense heartbreak I had endured over a two year period turned into a full-blown "incurable illness." Two heart attacks within six months signaled the end of life as I had known it. I was told I could debilitate quickly to death, but with small children I loved dearly, I chose life instead.

This one decision launched me on a search for a cure that would completely change my life and set me on a path to fulfill my Life Purpose. It was an exciting journey of discovery beyond what I could have known without this mortal challenge. It was my own personal quest deep into the heart of my illness and the many challenging circumstances that had long troubled me.

My passion for unlocking the Mystery of Self kept me going deeper. I was unraveling the mysteries of my life and waking up to the deeper truths that were waiting like jewels to be excavated beneath the layers of my human conditioning.

Finally, I stood at the doorway of the psyche, knowing that to be completely healed, I had to venture into the dark shadowed depths of that uncharted territory, for I had done everything I could to that point, but had not had a complete cure. The pioneering doctors I had studied and trained under with their cutting edge technologies had helped me not to debilitate any further, but I knew there was more. Another horizon was calling to me. It was the last frontier.

It is said that when we are ready, the teacher appears. This happened to me. It was 1991. A Kahuna in the Hawaiian Tradition stepped into my driveway. He said he had been drawn by the healing music. Within the next few days, he began transferring the most incredible Huna Healing Arts to me.

He was supposed to pass this Knowledge to someone in his family, he said, but he had seen my future. I would be helping people all over the world, and even though he was mainly focused on training others in martial arts, I was meant to be his Successor in the Kahuna Lineage. Thus began a series of incredible sessions with Hawaiian mystic and healer, Grandmaster Pang.

Grandmaster Pang traveled between Oahu and Portland where he ran his Shaolin Internal Systems martial arts schools. Each time he arrived on the island, he would come to see me. Immediately, I would be scanned from head to toe as he calmly spoke to me. Seeing that I was aware of the scan, he would simply say, "I have to be careful! This knowledge cannot be passed to someone who would misuse it." Passing his test, I would receive the next training, which would be an inner journey to the heart of the wounds I had been carrying but never knew existed.

What was so amazing was that after each visit with the Kahuna, sessions with my clients would be on a whole new level. My inner sight would be opened to a greater degree and my healing abilities would be far beyond what they had been before.

One of the most powerful healing arts he passed to me was the Ho'oponopono. This ritual of forgiveness releases us from the heavy burden we're carrying from of our past that causes us to feel old, tired, and worn out. This includes painful memories, traumatic experiences, and scarring from the judgments of others.

One session is a complete life clearing. We start at the present and work our way back to birth or before, healing each memory and negative dynamic with others. The work can take one hour or five, depending on one's life history, but must be continued until everything is complete. People have tremendous life changes as the weight of the past is released along with guilt, self-judgments, and shame. Relationships can then flourish and the person feels more their Authentic Self.

This training was invaluable to the development of TheQuest. Having experienced the deepest levels of healings, I wanted that for others.

Releasing negative emotions from painful situations is important. Aka cords, which in the Huna Tradition tie us to others, drain our energy and keep us in a negative dynamic with them. Grandmaster Pang said that the ancient Kahunas likened us to bowls of light that accumulate stones from our painful life experiences. These stones must be continually removed for us to be our best selves, thus the importance of practicing Ho'oponopono.

In a Sacred Ceremony on my birthday in 1993, Grandmaster Pang passed his Kahuna Lineage and Mana (Healing Energy) to me, graduating me as a Kahuna. This was a powerful conclusion to an extraordinary experience that had gifted me with an important key to understanding the psyche.

CHAPTER FIVE

Journey Into the Shadow Lands

It was the timely meeting with Grand Master Pang that had opened the doorway to the psyche, a whole new and exciting world I didn't know existed. It was there I found a powerful part of me, a wounded inner child the Kahunas call the Unihipili that was continually sabotaging everything I was striving for in my life.

Though I lived what could be called an exemplary life following the highest principles, my daily existence many times did not reflect the harmony and peace that should have been my life experience. Instead of reaping happiness and the fulfillment of my dreams, this shadow part of me was like a magnet, drawing in challenges that continually caused misery, suffering, and pain. It was these experiences that compelled me to find out why, and to see if there was a way to change the unhappy circumstances I was encountering. This one intention allowed me to unlock the deeper mysteries of my life and the dilemma that we must overcome if we are going to create a world of peace.

My journey led me to explore this Shadow Self and I came to understand how often I had been held in its grip. It had been a huge, yet subtle force, in my life that was continually holding me back and limiting my success. At times it would overwhelm me with upsets, anger, fear, or rage. It was driving me to be a workaholic while sabotaging my every effort. It was keeping me from realizing my full potential.

The Kahuna had taught me that there are three distinct parts to the human psyche. The Unihipili, which is our inner child or subconscious, the Uhane, which is our conscious self, and the Aumakua, which is our super conscious or higher self. While it is our Uhane that carries our everyday awareness, it is continually infected and run by our Unihipili. When this takes place, we are out of balance.

When we lose our poise and control, we also lose touch with our Aumakua, our higher awareness and the part of us that is always connected to our Source. So, we feel lost, fearful, separate, and alone. The choices we make are from an upset child that could be two, four, or even five years old, while our mature self has receded with its positive influence.

Out of control, our decisions fail to provide the outcome that would give us the greatest fulfillment and success in life, and we see this continually in the world. Angry reactions creating endless wars and enmity between nations until one can only wonder how old these people are who are running the countries of the world.

Mastering the Unihipili is an important aspect to Kahuna training. It is the Uhane, with the guidance of the Aumakua that must minister to the wounded inner children within us. When this is done, we become whole. We live in harmony and balance, and have inner peace. It is then our bowls of light can shine brightly.

Having been in the grip of the Unihipili too many times in my life, I was eager to lessen its power in my world. Gaining more control became my focus. The more inner journeying I did to the heart of my upsets, the more compassion I gained for the wounded children that were lurking in the shadowlands of my psyche, providing the great dramas, setbacks, devastation, and hardships in my life.

I was determined to find a way to overcome this handicap, and to change the circumstances of my life, rather than just clear the debris from the devastations I had experienced. This began my most landmark research and work in the psyche. Each trek into those uncharted realms was significant and profound. Through this inner quest, I made many exciting discoveries that contradicted popular beliefs until at last, I discovered what I feel is a "missing piece" to our present earth dilemma.

CHAPTER SIX

Unlocking the Secret Code

Along with my training with the Kahuna, I had studied and applied many of the highest spiritual teachings available on the planet. Yet, I was still facing an illness I had not been able to completely cure. It was then that my personal quest brought me to the field of psychology. I entered an intensive period where I earned my B.A., M.A., and PhD.

From this training I realized how humanity, after millennia of unconscious living, heartbreaks, and wars, had been driven to find answers to their earthly dilemma in a whole new frontier. Thus began an exploration of the inner world of the soul.

Spiritual manuscripts throughout time have called us to live more consciously, to embody our higher nature and yet, we have not known how to quell the darker aspects of our personality, or to live in a continued enlightened state. We have not understood the true cause of suffering and so we have learned to suppress our dark nature rather than to heal it.

Finally, in the last century, the first pioneers in psychology discovered that when people air their feelings, they are able to deal more effectively with their personal challenges. Thus was born the psychiatrist couch. But airing feelings and resolving issues are two different things and soon it became evident that an inner process needed to take place to help facilitate a deeper resolution.

Person Centered Counseling was developed by Dr. Carl Rogers, who found that by creating a caring atmosphere where he sat facing his client, they would feel safe to venture into a deep inner inquiry. He listened compassionately, reflected feelings, gave acknowledgment, and held in silence at appropriate moments. Finally, the client would unravel and solve their own problems, miraculously emerging confident and self-assured.

Another powerful step in understanding the psyche came through the work and collaboration of Wolfgang Köhler, a German psychologist and his colleagues, Max Wertheimer and Kurt Koffka, who together founded Gestalt psychology. They came to the realization that the part of us that is upset is actually an inner subconscious personality, similar to what the Kahunas understood in ancient Hawaii in their work with the Unihipili.

One Gestalt approach has the client move into a third chair where they become the voice of the upset part. In this way, the person can disassociate themselves enough from their feelings to be able to discern the part of them that is actually feeling this way so that it can be directly worked with.

During an extraordinary M.A. degree program at the University of Santa Monica (USM), I was able to master many of the cutting edge counseling theories and practices born of the last century. These included Gestalt, NLP, Person Centered Counseling, Reality Therapy, Psychosynthesis, and more. Through this training I was able to personally apply the techniques I was learning, which took me deeper into the causes behind my illness, and helped me make sense of the challenging life conditions I had endured.

Once I earned my doctorate, I continued my research directly in the psyche through Self Counseling sessions as well as by working with my family, friends, and clients. I was bent on solving the mystery behind the challenges that seem to be an inescapable part of our earthly existence, and this helped paved the way to developing a Life Mastery Path that I found both empowering and life changing. I was traversing a new frontier, unlocking mysteries still undiscovered by most of humanity. I was excavating the deep layers of the psyche on a Quest for Truth, and I was making landmark discoveries. My own personal challenges were the catalyst that continually drove me on.

Like many people in this world, I had followed spiritual models that should have ensured me a life of ease. When faced with immense challenges that seemed incurable or unchangeable, I would immediately apply these higher principles, but sometimes to no avail. I would strive to move into peace while a part of me still seethed with resentment and anger. The more I tried to force these feelings down or to spiritually bypass them, the stronger they would become. I would lose my temper and then feel guilty or ashamed. I had self-judgment rather than compassion for myself, because I had been taught that feeling or behaving this way is bad.

Strive as I might, I could not seem to change the negative dynamics in my relationships. No amount of positive thinking or trying to coerce myself into being content with the way things were would change the disappointment I felt in my marriage. I could try to forgive people, but it was hard to like a person who had betrayed me and when I strove to be loving and kind to those who had harmed or wronged me, I felt like I was betraying myself.

These experiences puzzled me because they were contrary to what I imagined would be the outcome of my spiritual practices. This compelled me to find out why, driving me deeper for answers until at last, I found the secret.

It was not that I was a sinner who could never be good, and so had to continually pay for my sins by reaping what I had sown. There was not an innately evil part of me that was stronger than the "good" part, leaving me helpless and in need of a spiritual remedy, a salvation that only someone or something outside of myself could bring. And at last, to my great relief, I found that I was not evil at my core. Yes, there were two very distinct and powerful parts of me, an enlightened, noble, peaceful self and a wounded, troubled "shadow" self, each affecting me in completely opposite ways, but the Shadow Self was not the innate part of me, neither did it have more power. It did have the ability to over-run my conscious awareness, however, and cloud my higher nature and this had been a troubling factor in my quest for spiritual attainment. Mastering this part of me became the next important step on my journey.

I found that when I was in my illumined, wise self, I was calm, peaceful and content. This self lived at the core of my being. Strong, powerful, and clear, it was directing my life. It was the inner fire that had inspired my quest for truth. Through many direct experiences with this Self, I was surprised to find that it had been unharmed by anything I had ever gone through. No matter what mistakes I had made, or how far I had plummeted from my ideals, it remained innocent, pure, and untainted.

This Self became a bastion of hope, a place of peace that I could enter and be restored. It had a wisdom that was profound, that could skillfully guide me through the twists and turns of life. Loving the deep inner peace I was tapping into, I was compelled to live in this calm, clear reality more often, and to learn how to quiet the shadow voices so that I could listen and follow the guidance of my Inner Self unfailingly.

Through each life challenge, this Illumined Self was drawing me within to unlock the secret code of my identity, inspiring me to remove the overlays that were like clouds covering over the innate happiness and peace I had discovered. The key was to immediately realize when my Shadow Self was up rather than being engulfed in the emotional responses from my life experiences. Each time I would feel troubled, fearful, or angry, I would move swiftly into action to heal and resolve the part of me that was upset, and found that I could actually shorten the time of misery.

The brilliance of having gone through a series of devastations was that I discovered a way not only to bring myself from upset to peace very quickly, but to also take the next step in actually reprogramming the subconscious patterns that were creating these conditions. This became a landmark discovery in my work in the psyche.

Soon I was like a Houdini, skillfully releasing myself from each challenging situation. I released myself from histories of pain that were weighing me down, coloring my outlook on life, and causing health conditions and even aging. I had accessed the pain and patterns that caused my incurable illness and in healing them, I was completely cured. When a cardiologist checked my heart years later, there was no residue of the serious condition I had been through.

Each challenge furthered my quest in the psyche, resulting in a host of exciting discoveries, the threads of which were woven into a tapestry I could finally understand. At last I made sense of the mortal challenges I had faced and why the highest principles I was embodying had not averted or changed the challenging conditions in my life. I saw how I had been driven deeper to find the truth and in discovering a way out, to then have a gift for humanity.

The arduous trek through subconscious patterns, inner monsters and self-sabotage finally brought me to a place of self-mastery I am excited to share. The darkness of my earthly trek had actually been an Illumined Pathway through a series of Dark Nights designed to give me a body of knowledge and a level of Life Mastery that is now assisting people throughout the world to heal and transform their lives.

CHAPTER SEVEN

Rewriting Destiny

There comes a time when you must leave behind all that you have known and go where you have never gone before to find the Truth. This is TheQuest, a journey deep into the heart of your true soul identity.

TheQuest Life Mastery Path provides tools to heal everything that has stood in your way, covered over your true nature, and brings you an understanding of what is behind your life challenges. That is when the labyrinth of the soul opens up to reveal its greatest secrets so that you can unlock the mystery of self and stand firmly in your Truth. This is a lost treasure valuable beyond anything we could ever find in a transitory material world.

Through TheQuest, I unlocked the secret code of my True Identity and found answers to the very nature of my earthly existence. In doing this deep inner work, I was rewriting my destiny. Patterns of being abused, abandoned or betrayed dissolved and these experiences were eliminated from my life. I had changed the inner programming and thus, my future.

I became an adept at immediately healing and transforming each challenge, thus shortening the time that the experience would play out. Instead of being depressed, angry or sad for weeks, I could get through it in hours. I could even avert disasters, undoing them before they became full blown devastation. In some experiences, facing immense tidal waves of destruction, I was able to heal the causes from within and watch as my life miraculously changed. It was as if the tsunami that was ready to crash over and devastate my life had been transformed into a calm sea with gentle waves bringing blessings to my shore.

This helped me realize the greater picture of my work, that facing dire potentials on earth, humanity could emerge unscathed. In the midst of grand disasters, the patterns behind all the dire potentials we are facing can be healed and our world transformed.

With this new level of mastery, I began to get a glimpse of how important it was to anchor my knowledge in a practical way. If I could master living consciously, I could help others do the same. The key was to allow my Authentic Self more time in my daily reality.

As I cleared the inner debris, my life was shifting dramatically. I was drawing in healthier relationships that allowed me to flourish and was able to say no to those that were weighing me down or destroying my self-esteem. I was skillfully healing every wound I had been carrying. I could quickly reprogram each self-sabotaging pattern that was holding me back, diminishing my creative expression, and dampening my passion for life. I was clearing the immense weight I was unconsciously carrying which had become an ever-increasing burden.

I released myself from being tired of this earthly existence and regained an authentic smile. With it came a renewed awe of the wondrousness of life. I began to feel ageless, healing many of the causes of aging within me that had clung to my body and altered my physical health. Soon I was living in an exquisite youthful reality most of the time, an experience that continues to this day.

Through the process, I was developing and perfecting TheQuest. I distilled it into Seven Steps and tested it on a host of applications, seeing great success with addictions, abuse, depression, trauma, illness, health challenges, financial issues, weight problems, menopause, aging, destructive relationship dynamics, suicidal tendencies, and even violence. The people who were finding me had immense challenges and big pieces to heal. Consequently, I witnessed many lives completely transformed.

TheQuest has helped change the lives of youth at risk, abused men, women, and children, substance abusers and addicts, gamblers, people with serious illnesses, and weight issues including young girls with anorexia. I found that every issue can be resolved and every pattern healed. Contrary to prevailing planetary thought, we can change our personality traits, heal our addictions, and transform the challenging conditions in our lives. Leopards might not be able to change their spots, but humanity can change its patterns, and when they are healed, our destiny is rewritten.

We no longer need to be victims to our fate, tossed on the seas of life until we are brokenhearted, worn out, and ruined. I've been there and I've discovered not only how to heal the wounds of the past, but also how to live more fully in every moment with passion, excitement about life and a youthful aliveness. Many authors write about what they themselves are learning or striving to master. The difference with this body of work is that I have mastered my shadow through TheQuest Self Counseling, an essential key in TheQuest Life Mastery Path, a way of life I've found a great joy in training others in.

In the next chapters, I offer the secret formula of TheQuest. Simple in its application, it works like magic, immediately shifting the worst conditions into an experience of great learning and growth. It allows you to change the challenging circumstances in your life by healing the corresponding subconscious patterns. When you do this work, you move from victimhood to empowerment. You feel victorious as you overcome each addiction and pattern. You become skillful in clearing every upset as it enters your conscious awareness. When you work your self-healing process as each issue arises, you forge a way of life that becomes an essential part of your daily lifestyle and you feel happy and content more often.

TheQuest Self Counseling is a process of deep inquiry that leads you back to the peace of your true nature, the truth of who you are behind your upsets and patterns. By practicing this art, you can reach a level of mastery few on earth have attained and realize your greater potential. As you apply TheQuest in your daily life, you can become an inspiration to others.

Restoring each facet of your Diamond Self, your outer challenges resolve and peace becomes a way of life. Like the hundredth monkey effect, your inner shift has a rippling affect on the collective. When more of humanity embodies their innate perfection, peace will be restored on earth.

Part Two

The Quest

CHAPTER ONE

The Secret Formula

TheQuest is a breakthrough technology that has been time tested with great success on a host of applications from addictions to abuse and on numerous subjects including teens and youth at risk. It has made a difference in the lives of addicts, abusers, people with health and other serious conditions including anxiety, depression, suicidal tendencies, grief, and trauma, and children and adults who were abused or had great losses. It has successfully healed a wide range of personality traits and dysfunctions. I continually see complete healings and transformed lives from this work and miracles happen all the time.

One miracle took place at my first Life Mastery Training Course in Aspen. I gave a woman a counseling session that took her back into forgotten memories where she had been severely abused. The next day she called me very excited saying a life long debilitation had been healed.

She writes, "I had pronated knees since I was a little girl. Continually aggravating the condition through a very active and full life, it became a life long affliction. By 25 years old I had to stop running, a great passion in my life. I also loved to ski, hike, and bike, but my knees would get so sore that my lifestyle was greatly hindered. At TheQuest Training in Aspen, I had the opportunity to work with Dr. Ariel. In my session we traced a pattern back to early childhood where I had suffered severe abuse. As we unlocked and healed the pattern, I felt a tremendous release. The very next day I was working out at the Aspen Club gym when, looking in the mirror, I noticed my legs were straight. My trainer came over and could hardly believe his eyes. The condition was healed!"

Her condition was a direct result of a wounded inner child, who having been violated and betrayed by someone close to her, had contracted into a protective posture that literally reformed her legs and made them turn inward. When the inner child was healed, she felt safe enough to trust again and was able to open fully. Immediately the physical condition she was holding in place dropped away and her legs straightened out. They no longer needed to turn inward to protect her.

I see this all the time with physical conditions that many believe must only be treated on the physical level when the true cause is found within. When you work on this deeper level, you not only change the condition you are facing, you eradicate it from your future. By healing the cause in the past, you stop the pattern in the present, and prevent its return in the future.

One woman came to me in great pain. She was a yoga teacher who had suffered a hip problem for months. No amount of rest, massage, or other outer methods would relieve it because the cause needed to be found inside her. The Inner Aspect that was holding this condition in place needed her full attention before she could release the physical condition. After one session, this woman was surprised to find she was no longer in pain. We had gotten to the heart of her condition by tracing it back to her early childhood and the beliefs she had taken on. Her Inner Aspect then released the pattern and her physical body immediately followed.

A client was on his way to the chiropractor one day. He was in serious pain with his hip out. I could see that it was about two inches out from where it should have been. We began looking more deeply into what this was about and that led us into TheQuest Seven Steps. Twenty minutes into the session, I witnessed his hip miraculously move back into place. Needless to say, there was no chiropractor visit that day. We had gotten to the heart of the problem and the condition was healed.

A woman with a severe case of emphysema came to me when she was first released from the hospital. After the first session she no longer needed her oxygen bottle. When she went to see her doctor, he was surprised at her unexpected return to health and also took her off her medication. After two sessions with me, her doctor could not believe she had quit smoking. He had been her doctor for the thirty years she had smoked and twenty of those years he had witnessed her trying to quit. Our work together simply got to the reason why she was smoking. Once we healed the part of her that needed to smoke, she was free of the addiction and craving.

When the lungs are afflicted, there is a story of grief that is usually tied in. In this woman's case, she had lost her ranch in a foreclosure, her father and her dog had died, and she had gotten a divorce all within a year. Soon after, she landed in the hospital. By getting to the heart of her grief and healing the causes behind her illness, she quickly returned to health. Had she not done this deeper work, she may very well have fulfilled her illness's death sentence.

A greatly significant piece to this work is how it can change lives dramatically. When we are released from patterns that drive us to be a certain way, we can live a life that is more in accord with our True Nature. One example was a teen in Aspen who was a troubled Youth At Risk. He was using drugs and alcohol and had been arrested five times. He was on probation and was continually in trouble at school.

He began coming to our weekly Teen Forum with his friends. My son, Aradeus, who was the same age, inspired him to get a private session from me. In that session, I found that this beautiful boy not only had a bleak outlook on life, but a very dark future. He could not see anything beyond further arrests and getting into trouble. He had been estranged from his alcoholic mother and lived with a verbally abusive father who also used cocaine and other drugs. His self-esteem was low and his self-confidence shot. A bright future was beyond this teen's comprehension.

Our session went deep into the cause behind his acting out and healed it. Immediately, in that moment, his future changed. By the end of the session he became passionate about exploring a career in marine biology and said he was committed to doing better in school so that he could get into a better college. That was the day his arrests and trouble at school stopped. His father saw a huge change in him and was surprised to find out that his son was attending our Teen Forum on his own. He called to thank me and told other parents about it who he thought should send their teens.

This boy's court appointed counselor was so amazed by his sudden and complete turn around she wrote, "When meeting with a court-ordered youth, I noticed an enormous shift in his attitude and responsibility in a very short period of time. So I asked him 'What has happened to cause you to mature so quickly?' That's when he told me that he was in a program for teens that was making a huge difference for him. I have not seen such a huge internal shift in a youth like this in a very long time. My interest in the TheQuest came from seeing results, not from hearing about the program. This is fantastic work!"

Sometimes the outer shift I see is miraculous, at other times the individual must go through a series of sessions to unlock the complete puzzle to a life challenge. This becomes a journey of self-discovery that is incredibly empowering. I see this many times with serious illnesses like the incurable heart condition I cured, and with people who have addictions or conditions like cancer. The psyche (the soul) is not seeking the cure of a moment. It needs time. It wants a complete lifestyle change from the inside out and to have that, it must first release the patterns that are directly related to the old lifestyle and to the way of being that brought the illness on.

There is a chemical process that takes place within us when we are imprinted with human programming that changes the very nature of our physical body. That is why you can trace every challenging condition to its origin within the psyche. To heal a serious illness or debilitating condition can take a series of TheQuest sessions supported by restructuring your lifestyle to foster health and well being, which can include products and modalities to help release the disease and restore the body.

Serious conditions, whether an illness or other physical condition, must be addressed on this deep level otherwise it may be cured or resolved in the present, only to return in the future. You want to heal your life challenges on the deepest levels, getting right to the core. By eradicating the root cause of your condition, the physical aspect can more easily be transformed.

Dr. Wayne Topping of the Topping International Institute found that when individuals work with their personal psychology in a constructive and effective way, they experience deeper levels of well being, happiness, and peace. Dr. Topping's work was part of my early foundational training. It gave me the understanding that there was a deeper cause behind my "incurable" illness, which inspired my journey within to find what was really at the heart of my condition. His landmark research into emotions and their effect on physical organs helped me trace what was behind my heart condition and the two heart attacks I had within six months. This led me to the heartbreak that had caused my illness, an important key on my journey to health.

Our challenges are opportunities for great growth and learning. They set us on a journey we might never have embarked upon. Fearing the worst, we access an inner strength that might not have been there before. Being overcome by challenges, we find skills we didn't know we had. Facing death, we come to appreciate life more reverently.

When we are dying, we want to live. The moment we face our darkest hour, we turn to the light. When we're held in the grip of an illness or debilitating physical condition, we seek health. When we are constrained by our finances, we seek freedom and relief. Our inner self kicks in and takes command. That is the physics of this soul journey. When you have the secret formula to unlock your life situations from within, challenges that once seemed insurmountable or conditions that felt unchangeable are easy to shift.

Many times a client will come to me feeling they can no longer take it. They've tried everything to no avail. When I tell them, "Don't worry, it's a piece of cake," they look at me in disbelief. This work is so cutting-edge that most people on the planet cannot imagine that there is relief like this available. They suffer on with their addictions, they feel relegated to being overweight, they can't imagine living without tension and stress.

One client wrote, "My heart is so open and full from this work. Being gently led through the deepest, darkest places leaves only gratitude, love and freedom. In every session we come quickly to the taproot of the issue, create safety for its exposure and transformation, and watch the magic with awe as the entire tree is healed. This work helps me feel so purposeful. I am proud to be a human, finally. The tools that Dr. Ariel uses for healing are pure magic, like laser surgery for the soul. The operation is fast, relatively painless and totally effective. People would not choose to live with pain if they knew this was available."

Each session is an incredible journey of discovery taking you to the heart of your life challenges and healing them from within. When the pattern is healed, you emerge victorious and feel empowered and free. It is then you realize how affected you were by your patterns and how they had held you in their grip. Sometimes you are being suffocated by your subconscious patterns and you don't even know it. You've lived with them so long they have become a normal way of life. You don't even realize you are in a prison.

There is a freedom and peace that is available to you but you will never realize it until you begin delving deeper into what is really going on in your life and face how you really feel about it. When you systematically extricate yourself from everything that is holding you back and limiting your creative expression, you set yourself free from what could have been a life sentence.

A Real Estate Broker in Denver wrote, "After years of being in and out of therapy I had changed my life very little, but after four sessions with Dr. Ariel, I was a new person. I had come to the first session a skeptic, but by the time we were done I was totally amazed by the amount of healing that took place. I had been hitting my head against the wall, not getting any movement in my years of therapy. Traditional therapy had only scratched the surface, whereas TheQuest dove right into the root of the issue, uncovered the truth, and healed that aspect of my inner self. The sessions have been the most powerful events in my life—I'm finally free of the unhealthy part of myself that was holding me back for years. I never thought transformation like this was truly possible. I'm no longer a victim of the past and my emotional traumas have been set free. I have my life back! I've made more progress in a few TheQuest sessions with Dr. Ariel than I have in years of therapy."

While miracles are commonplace with TheQuest, some conditions require that you take time to unlock each piece of the puzzle. In that way, you gain a conscious awareness of a complex pattern that is responsible for your challenging condition. Your life can miraculously change in one session, or you may be on a healing journey that can take months or even a year. Whatever the time period for your complete release, it will definitely be an insightful and rewarding journey.

By applying TheQuest Self Counseling, you can change your life. You can step free of your addictions. You can lose weight and live a healthy life. You can heal the causes behind your anxiety and be released from tension and stress. When you tend to the deeper conditions in your life, there is a self-nurturing aspect that is very comforting. You begin relaxing and finally, you sink into an exquisite peace. Your life situations are resolved and you are released from their prison. Very quickly, you come to understand what has been behind the challenges you have faced. This helps you have more compassion for yourself and others.

We're in an age of miracles where everything can change in a twinkling of an eye. With TheQuest Master Keys we can turn everything around. We can undo millennia of human programming and step free to realize our full potential. We can bring our Authentic Self into the equation of impending planetary demise and witness the shift of the ages, moving instead into a Golden Age. As we journey through this historic time, miraculous changes are taking place within the psyche of humanity and we are all a part of this. We are in a state of rapid evolution, breaking free of the confines that left us limited and living so much less than our potential.

CHAPTER TWO

The Wounds From Your Past Can Be Healed

Working with clients over the years, I began to realize that the only people who ever seemed to "find me" were people who had great hurdles to overcome. Drawn to the deep, powerful transformation TheQuest work provides, they were on a Quest for Peace. Through our sessions, I watched as these people completely changed their lives. No one showed up who wanted to just scratch the surface of his or her life challenges. Neither did this work seem to draw those who were content to remain victims to their life circumstances.

The people who were coming to do this work were committed to freeing themselves from unhealed wounds, to unlocking themselves from the prison of challenging relationship dynamics, to ending an addiction or cycle of abuse. These people were intent on creating a different reality and found to do that, they had to go within and change their subconscious programming. To alter their course and change their future, they had to address the patterns that were keeping them in a limited or painful existence. These have been people who had a greater purpose to fulfill, but who were entangled in their human patterns. Some became students with the intention that, as future TheQuest Counselors, they would make a difference in other people's lives. Others have the potential to be powerful catalysts in world affairs.

As these people came for healing, I saw miracles take place in their lives and in each session, a similar story emerged. It became evident that each person had an important destiny to fulfill but was entangled in challenging life circumstances reflective of their subconscious patterns. While each client shared a similar vision of a world transformed and had a glimpse of how they wanted to help, their own personal dramas and personality dysfunctions stood in the way. They were trapped in painful relationship dynamics, had challenging financial issues, or were dealing with scary health problems. Ensnared by earthly circumstance, their vision of a better life was salt in the wound of their present limiting experience.

As we traced the patterns that were at the heart of their life challenges, the same information would be revealed. These people had determined to be born into challenging circumstances, to be wounded by life experiences, or to go through particular trials in life so that they would have something to overcome, be catalyzed on a quest for healing and truth, or be compelled to go deeper into questions about themselves in a quest for their true identity. All of this was for one purpose, so that in finding a way out, an inner resolution to their own "soul dilemma," they would have a gift for humanity. By walking the veil of tears of this world, they would have an empathy and compassion for others. I found this amazing!

There is a reason behind all the madness! The chaos of our world is not only reflective of unhealed aspects in the psyche of humanity, but the way out is an incredible journey to restore the innate design of our inner world. When we do this inner work, we bring our unique gifts and talents to the equation and we change the world around us. Through many profound sessions the same story was revealed. I began to realize that there were many souls who had come to earth for a similar purpose, to help humanity at this crucial time. While I had witnessed the awakening taking place over the years, I had not understood this important element. Many souls, destined to help the planet move into a positive future, had not chosen to come to earth as enlightened beings but rather, had embodied into a host of painful circumstances so that they could understand the dilemmas of humanity, have compassion and care, and be catalyzed on a quest for healing that would assist them to awaken to their life's purpose.

I've seen this with substance abusers, who in healing and transforming their own lives, had forged a special gift for those who were similarly afflicted; with women who were sexually abused as children who now had an ability to help other women and children; and with people who had gone through financial trials who now had a rare understanding and talent for helping others in financial difficulty. Whatever wounds of the past were being healed, whatever hardships had been endured, these were signs of their future areas of service.

Witnessing the many miracles of TheQuest over the years has given me hope for humanity and a vision that we can turn the tide on present planetary affairs and enter an era of peace. But first, we must find peace within and to do that, we need to embrace and get comfortable with our shadow. Instead of recoiling at the first sign of an emotional response, we must follow our feelings down into the heart of our core pain and undo the programming there. That is when the magic of TheQuest can quickly transform our lives from within.

Through TheQuest, you can clear the past and change the behaviors that have created havoc in your life. Even if you've become a serious drug addict, been abusive to your mate, violent with your children, or are just plain unhappy, you can change your life. Through healing the wounded aspects in your subconscious, you can live more joyously with a heart that is wide open rather than being shut down, fearful, or contracted in pain. This creates an awakening in consciousness that can catalyze you to contribute to our present earth equation in a phenomenal and powerful way. All the troubles you've gone through, all the challenges, set backs, and hardships will have made sense, giving you a compassionate heart that can now help others.

An Inner Alchemy takes place when you apply this counseling technique to your life issues. It is such a powerful experience to feel the transformation you go through during each Self Counseling session. It is as if the cells and atoms of your life are rearranged and restored to their innate perfection and you step forth into a New Reality and whole new life, feeling renewed and inspired. This powerful transfiguration affects not only your mental, emotional, and physical health, but your physical reality as well.

When my son, Aradeus, hit his teen years, he found this work very helpful. It allowed him to delve deeply into his issues and feelings, and to clear an early traumatic history that could have tainted his whole life. Aradeus began receiving sessions at sixteen when he first encountered the normal challenges and self esteem issues that come with the teen years and this work altered his future. He stepped free of patterns that would have created a very different life had he not done this work.

It has been an amazing experience watching him move through the family patterning of his early years into a confidence and clarity as he approaches manhood. Already, he has brought the profound wisdom he has gained from his own inner trek to countless kids his age, helping them positively change their lives.

Aradeus wrote, "TheQuest is a great way to get things off your chest and deal with feelings that have been deep inside and yet are affecting you in a negative way. It really works!" Because he has suffered through his own life challenges and wrestled with his own inner patterns, he has a compassionate understanding of others, which is rare at his age. Usually it is through a lifetime of experiences that we gain the wise insightfulness of the elders that we can then pass on to others. It's incredible to witness someone in their early adulthood, garnishing the wisdom of the ages from his early trek into the wilderland to uncover life's deepest mysteries.

His journey has given me hope for the youth of the world. As he has systematically extricated himself from a wounding inherent in his family lineage and the scars he received through challenging experiences in his youth, he has proven a way for other young people to arrive at adulthood with a clear understanding of their life purpose, value, and worth. Instead of emerging into a society of adults similarly wounded, our teens and young adults now have a very real capacity to transform the wounds of their past into a very needed service to humanity.

The scars of our past can be healed at a young age. Aradeus has proven this! By the time he was nineteen, he had trained in TheQuest for a year and a half and had become an extraordinary counselor. Some of my most treasured experiences have been our back-to-back counseling sessions where we assisted each other with the challenges we were each facing in our lives.

My journey with Aradeus has been a profound experience. Our connection is a mother/son archetype that many shamans, healers, and medicine people have shared in the past, as they passed their sacred knowledge to the successor in the family. Aradeus is a Kahuna in training in TheQuest Tradition and I am excited to see how this will translate into his unique purpose in this life.

It's been an incredible joy to pass my knowledge to him, to my daughter, Mariah, and to my other children, and to share this deep, sacred journey with them. Today, many people can embody this special relationship with their children when they adopt TheQuest Life Mastery Path and walk this victorious pathway with them.

Aradeus was the one who saved me from the terrible Tsunami that hit Indonesia, Thailand, and India. It was December 2004. I had spent the summer in Aspen with him and returned alone to Maui as he went out on his own. I was preparing to go to Thailand after Christmas for the winter to complete my first book, when I kept feeling Aradeus's heart calling to me.

I have a very deep connection with all four children and have been highly attuned to their needs, even across great distances. At one period my son Gabriel, who was young at the time, could get me to call him within minutes. We would always laugh about it. I would feel that he needed me and sure enough, he would. I would always ask, "How long did it take me to call this time?" And it was sometimes only a minute. Somehow I can always feel how my children are doing and this is not always easy. No one told me that by having four children I'd be living five embodiments at once, feeling every single bump in the road as if I was personally living them! When two or more are troubled the weight can be quite commanding but when they are all doing well, it's like heaven on earth!

When I kept feeling Aradeus so strongly, I tuned in and realized that he was literally drawing me into a very different future. Curious, I called him to find out what was going on. I told him, "I'm really excited about going to Thailand to finish the book, but I keep feeling your heart calling me back to Aspen. When I look at the whole world, it's dark and the only light is coming from you. Somehow your heart is beckoning to me so strongly, I feel like the only place I want to be in the world right now is with you. And, you're in Aspen and it's winter!"

His response amazed me. He said that he needed to train in my work, TheQuest, and that he felt it had something to do with his destiny, that somehow in the future he would be bringing out his own piece, his own work, and this training was important for him. Without a second thought, I booked my flight to Aspen, packed up my belongings and shipped them and my car to the winter lands of Colorado, and arrived in Aspen December 21st in time to spend Christmas with him. Days later, a Tsunami devastated the island in Thailand where I would have been living. Aradeus's heart, which had called to me over the distance, had very possibly saved my life and allowed me to be sharing this work with you today.

So began an incredible year of weekly back-to-back counseling sessions where I was training him in becoming a Master Counselor. One time we sat in the sun on a picnic bench surrounded by snow, overlooking the town of Aspen. It was there he helped me clear a pattern of financial constraint. Within a week, I received a $2000 check in the mail from an unexpected source. This is the kind of magic I see all the time with TheQuest. When we clear the inner dynamic, our outer reality shifts accordingly. It is truly an effortless way to deal with life challenges, so much less arduous than what people feel they must do to handle their challenging circumstances.

People close to me have always marveled how many miracles happen to me. I can be in the worst circumstance or situation financially and in the next moment, everything works out miraculously and I am fine. I just go within and change the movie. Now, no matter what I go through, I can never receive any sympathy from my children, even if I am facing something scary. They simply say, "You know a miracle is coming, so why be concerned?" I always answer, "Because I don't know what is going to happen to me." We see so many trials in the outer world. It's easy to imagine the worst, but time and time again, TheQuest works its miracle and the challenge turns into a blessing. So, my children always end up right.

We've been taught to work harder and faster when facing challenges, but having had many serious challenges to overcome, I found that doing the inner work first is more effective. When you clear the patterns that are in charge of your discomfort and free yourself from the emotional response to the situation, which can be debilitating in itself, you have greater clarity that allows you to take positive action steps that are wise, empowered, and directed. It's amazing how fast the circumstances in our life can change from this inner work.

The knowledge Aradeus gained, along with the incredible experience of working effectively with his own psychology, an essential part of TheQuest Life Mastery training, is something that is available to all our youth. Aradeus represents a new generation of souls who may very well go far beyond our own capacity to realize their full potential at a young age.

When I think of all the misery, suffering, and dysfunctional relationships Aradeus is eliminating from his future by addressing and healing his patterns early on, I feel hopeful that our world can be turned around, as more of our youth take their lives into their own hands by healing the schisms in their psychology. The conditions many are born into are severe, but if they apply this work, their futures can be bright and meaningful. No one needs to be ruined. Now the deep scars that once etched their images across countless lives can be removed and their True Identity restored. Everyone can live a purposeful, fruitful life.

No matter what you've gone through, no matter what you've endured, you can cleanse yourself of painful memories. You can extricate yourself from life sentences that became prisons. You can remove the stains and feel good about yourself. You can create a life of tranquility and experience a deep inner peace. This is a quality inherent in the human psyche. The overlays in your personality may have kept you away from this peace, but it is still right within you. Accessing and living from this peace is a Life Mastery Art that is attainable, no matter what the challenge or circumstance.

The power of TheQuest is its ability to transform the inner structures that create and hold your challenging life circumstances in place. It is a powerful process of release that can help you let go of the past, resolve your deep issues, and clear the residue of pain that lies like a swamp within the caverns of the psyche.

Jack Canfield, author of Success Principles and co-author of the Chicken Soup For The Soul Series wrote about the powerful shifts that occur through TheQuest saying, "TheQuest session with Aurora unblocked a subtle, but powerful limitation in my life. I am grateful to her for her work and for her safe and gentle way of being."

Through every challenge, peace is calling to you. It wants to enfold you in its warm, vibrant presence until all your fears, heartache, and pain are gone. It longs to return you to your natural peaceful self, the true you behind all the patterns.

As each layer of this subconscious patterning is transformed, the outer follows in obedience. You emerge your radiant Wise Self, with the ability to set clear boundaries, make better decisions, and create more harmony in your life.

When you heal your patterns, you change your destiny. That is when miraculous changes can take place in your life. When you heal workaholic patterns, you create more time for yourself and thus, have a more quality life. When you heal controlling patterns, you make room for synchronicities to take place and you begin to experience the magic of life. When you heal the pain and sorrow that has clung to you since your childhood, constricting your body and etching its hardness into your facial features, you become more alive. When you heal overwhelm, you can breathe free and move forward unfettered.

A brilliant author and real estate broker in Hawaii wrote of his release from a major martyr pattern saying, "I feel differently. My attitude has changed. I definitely have transcended my pattern. I am a whole new being! TheQuest session was like an exorcism, casting a demon out of my being that was like a leach, sucking the life force out of me, and preventing me from being who I am as a person. After one session, I am a completely different person."

This Inner Alchemy is an important key for overcoming your past and moving into a glorious future. It is an essential element in creating a more rewarding and fulfilling life. It is the quintessential ingredient you need to have peace of mind.

It is very important for those who are destined to be of service, for your life may be more challenging than others. Many people who have an important destiny to fulfill must first face severe conditions. The alcoholic who has made it out safely now has a special gift and knowledge to give others. The abused child, successful in healing her wounds, now has something valuable to share with the world. But first, each must find a way out of these conditions before they can bring their gift to the world.

It has been the same for Aradeus and me. We've had to pass through many excruciatingly painful experiences that worked their magic in calling us to fulfill a higher destiny potential than what our patterns would have dictated. These challenges compelled us to find a way out of the misery, a way to clear the overlays that were laying like heavy weights upon our souls, clouding our judgment and polluting our outlook on life. The challenges we've faced have given us a greater interest in the troubles of others and a compassionate understanding of what people are going through, and this compassion has compelled us to make a difference. Had we been born without a care in the world, in circumstances that kept us apart from and out of touch with suffering in this world, we would never have been compelled to do this inner work, nor would we be able to truly understand what others go through.

All my children have received sessions through the years. This has helped them to go deep within to heal patterns that would have adversely affected their futures and because of this work, they have a very keen understanding of the psyche. This is something we can pass down to the children of the world. It is my dream that this training will be given to youth in high schools all over the planet, and to young adults in college. It can work wonders in prison reform, addiction, and youth at risk programs. Providing the "missing piece," it is a technology that can change lives and end the reign of suffering that has traversed family lines for millennia.

Virginia, a nurse manager now living in Hawaii shared, "TheQuest process is awesome. I have been through a lot of counseling since the age of 18. I knew as an adult child of alcoholics, without a good role model, I was going to need guidance to overcome my past even at that young age. As a nurse, I have also been exposed to mental heath treatment methods in my career. I have never experienced anything as impressive and empowering."

When we become masters of our psychology we enter a glorious pathway of enlightenment, freedom, and peace. We have tools to transform every dark night into a glorious day. We can handle anything that ever comes up in our life with an expertise and skill that is rare. In addressing life issues on all levels, mental, physical to subconscious, we can pull the plug on challenging life circumstances and watch them miraculously change before our eyes. This is the level of mastery the New Millennium is calling for if we are going to change the dire conditions we are facing with and create a better world.

CHAPTER THREE

TheQuest Life Mastery Path

Mastering the Art of Self Counseling is an important Key to Inner Peace. The more adept you become at this, the more you will be your Authentic Self, experiencing a sense of freedom, happiness, fulfillment, and joy. The key is to do TheQuest Seven Steps as issues arise, rather than suppressing your upset or wrestling with your feelings while being completely overcome and run by them.

So, how can you masterfully traverse challenging conditions and still maintain a level of composure and your creative edge? How can you deal with the phantoms that rise without warning from the dark recesses of your psyche and hold to a sense of equanimity and grace? How can you manage your anger while maintaining loving relationships?

Understanding this dilemma, I was inspired to release my work to the lay person rather than just giving it to practitioners as is normally done when a Counseling Theory and Healing Practice is developed. I realized that if I distilled my practice into a Self Counseling Technique that was easy to apply, it would give people the ability to deal with their issues in a timely way. I was excited by the idea that many more people than I could assist personally would be able to experience profound healings and be able to do this inner work in the privacy of their own homes.

For years I had done my own Self Counseling sessions. This work was empowering, taking me through some very challenging times. Others around me would be amazed. How could I go from being that upset to calm, peaceful, and clear in less than an hour! This was an area of mastery no one had heard of.

It was my son, Aradeus, who insisted I translate TheQuest counseling technique into seven steps, so that he could give the format to the teens in the weekly Teen Forum he and I were co-facilitating. So, I wrote them out and what we saw was amazing! The kids loved it and some of them actually ran with it and changed their lives! One 15 year old, who attended a progressive school, was able to use TheQuest Journal of Self Counseling sessions to fulfill one of her course requirements. The school was so impressed they invited Aradeus and me to present this work to her whole class.

During that time, I was also invited to present TheQuest to two classes at Aspen High School where I took the teens and their teacher through the Seven Steps. The response was incredible. In one class, the teacher was very concerned about how I would be received. He said, "This is an unruly bunch of kids. They don't pay attention and they can be extremely rude." Imagine his surprise when the kids in his class were riveted by the information the whole hour and a half and not only that; they all did their Self Counseling with the Seven Steps, many of them sharing their process with the class after each step.

At one point, the supposedly "coolest" kid in the school went to the blackboard, drew his Inner Aspect and began writing his feelings on the board while the other students supported him with suggestions. The teacher was stunned!

In his letter of recommendation the teacher wrote, "I have to admit that I was a bit skeptical how this would play out to a group of 20 or so usually somewhat inattentive high school students. Both classes were surprisingly attentive and interested in what Dr. Ariel presented. The fact that she held everyone's attention with something that was somewhat foreign to all of these students and she had all the class thank her as she left for the day and others asking for more, told me that she was on the right track with the work she has dedicated her life to. I also followed along with the class in the exercises she had designed for that day and was amazed at the insights that were provided to me in so brief a period of time."

In the past, a Counseling Theory and Practice would be given to practitioners to apply with their clients. In this way, the community was served, but it didn't address the greater problem, that humans had no control or mastery over their psychology and therefore were unable to be wise stewards of their lives. Tossed by the sea of planetary challenge, it was a rare individual that could steer his or her ship quickly into clear waters. Most people are completely overwhelmed by challenging life circumstances. They do not have the tools to traverse them with skill. To handle situations, many will bury their feelings and then will later become ill or will "lose" their tempers, ruining relationships or chances of advancement at work.

As I've watched the miracles of TheQuest in my own life and the lives of my children, clients and students, I've wanted to share it with the world, to give it "to the people." That is why I always educate and train my clients while I am working with them. I have such a strong sense that it is important to pass on this knowledge, to help people understand their psychology, and to give them the tools to change their lives.

One client in Hawaii wrote, "Gone are the days of long drawn out traditional therapies. With TheQuest I have found a way to heal and transform any pattern or history from ancient to present times. I have found a new sense of purpose in life with each healing of the darker aspects of myself, a greater love for all that I am. TheQuest allows me to address issues as they come up and access the core of the issue to transform it all in one session! Aurora's dedication to the healing arts has empowered me as a wife, mother, businesswoman, healer, and human being." It is responses like these that have kept the fire burning inside of me to bring this work to everyone it is meant for!

TheQuest Life Mastery Path is simple. The moment that an issue is up, when you feel distraught, angry or upset, it is time for TheQuest Self Counseling. The sooner you get to this work, the faster you will have your issue resolved. In this way, you shorten the time of misery, and return to the harmony and peace of your True Nature quickly.

If you want to traverse your life and display the greatest mastery, you must address your issues as they arise. Following the Seven Steps, you can facilitate your own Self Counseling process, tracing your feelings to the part of you that is calling for attention and healing. By applying the Seven Steps, you can move yourself quickly from upset to peace, while healing a pattern that has contributed to the challenging condition in your life. You can do this in a journal format writing out your answers, and then once you master this technique, you can do the Seven Steps as a self-guided inner process.

Preparing for your Self Counseling session is important.

In the following chapters, I give you steps that will help you create a safe space that will allow you to go to the deepest levels in your healing and I lay out TheQuest Seven Steps. As you learn this Art of Self Counseling, it is best to use a journal. In this way, you will be able to stay on track with your session from beginning to end and have a record of the healing that took place to review in the future.

Becoming proficient in this work, you become a Master of your Psychology, working on important elements in your psychological makeup and healing them as they arise. With each Self Counseling session you feel more whole and complete.

As you restore each imperfect facet of your personality to its innate design, you tap into the awesome power of your Authentic Self and give it the power to manifest its vision in your life. No longer run by your unconscious patterns, you heal your issues and transform your patterns as they come to your conscious awareness. By practicing the Art of Self Counseling in a timely way, you make the wisest choices for your life and fulfill your Highest Destiny Potential.

CHAPTER FOUR

Self Counseling With TheQuest

TheQuest Self Counseling is a way to go to the heart of life conditions, unlock them from within, and heal them for the last time. When you do this inner work, the outer world changes around you. As you learn to be more peaceful, the world will reflect your inner peace. This is how peace can be restored on Earth, one person at a time, and why I feel so excited to offer TheQuest as a remedy for a world in travail.

This powerful, cutting edge technique can change your life, because it works directly with the subconscious aspects in charge of your challenging life situations, transforming them from within. Mastering the Seven Steps, you become adept at freeing yourself from challenging circumstances. When you apply this technique, you have found a Master Key to Inner Peace.

Each time you free yourself from the grip of upset feelings you return to your True Nature, the part of you that is always calm, centered, and peaceful. When you learn how to set yourself free from every challenge and to resolve your issues quickly, you begin to experience an exquisite joy in your new freedom. Dealing with challenges quickly and effectively allows you to do the things you enjoy in life, and you are happier when you do them.

In each Self Counseling session, you are able to understand the challenges you've encountered, realize the great value and growth they brought to your life, and see how they assisted you in having more compassion for others. In finding a way out of each dilemma, you not only become a master of your life, you have developed a gift of greater awareness you can now share with others. In overcoming life challenges in this masterful way, you gain a unique insight into your psychology and healing patterns becomes an exciting journey of self-discovery and awakening.

How To Work Your Self Healing Process

When you feel upset or when you have an emotional response to something that happens in your life, it is time to do TheQuest Self Counseling. When you deal with your feelings on this deeper level, you resolve your issues quickly and you gain the clarity and insight needed to handle the situation effectively.

Self Counseling is an essential element of TheQuest Life Mastery Path. It provides the tools that allow you to gain control over your emotions and heal facets of your psychology that are sabotaging and holding you back. By working your Self Counseling as issues arise, you are able to return to a clear calm place where you can direct your life course more effectively.

TheQuest Seven Steps are designed to help you get to the heart of your upset feelings and resolve them quickly. When strong feelings arise, it is important that you feel your emotions fully, refraining from self-judgment. Being with your feelings helps you get in touch with what is really going on inside and will help you access the part of you that is feeling that way. Tending to this upset part in a timely way is important.

You may feel that the situation warrants a strong emotional response, so it is natural you would feel that way. But when you are upset you are not in the natural balance and flow of your True Nature, and actions and decisions fueled by these feelings can be destructive. It is extremely important to turn within when you get upset, because your feelings will lead you to a place inside that is calling for attention and healing. Ignoring your feelings will only delay the deeper resolution and healing that is available to you.

Your feelings are allies. They draw your awareness within to an upset aspect (subconscious personality) that was wounded or colored from the past. The event that triggered your emotional response activated this inner part of you. As its feelings come to your awareness, you are able to work with it.

What is important to know is that an Inner Aspect is never activated unless it is ready to be healed. Each time you are upset or become aware of a pattern, it is an opportunity for you to step free from a program that has limited or held you back. It is a call to change your life in an important way at the perfect time for your soul advancement.

When you do this inner work, the shift that occurs can be profound. By listening to your feelings and trusting this inner process, you are able to release yourself from the core pattern in charge of your situation and move to the next level of conscious awareness. When you emerge clear and centered, you are a commanding presence that is in charge of your life and destiny. You are no longer tossed on the sea of life without a rudder or clear direction to guide your way. You have returned to the clarity of your True Nature and to your authentic power.

In **Step One**, it is important to step back into a "witness" point of view once you have fully felt your feelings. In this way, you can see the part of you that is upset and work with it directly. Many people believe they are the upset part, so it is hard for them to distinguish that only a part of them is feeling this way. The truth is, there are many facets to the personality. You can have many conflicting parts. For example, you might feel very angry but at the same moment, you may also think the situation is not worth getting upset about. You may have a part of you that hates someone, while another part feels guilty and ashamed for feeling that way. One part may be tired and worn out, while another part feels like it must drive you onward.

Stepping back and centering in your Authentic Self, the neutral observer that continually witnesses your life from a calm clear bastion of peace, allows you to work effectively with the part of you that is upset. You want to help it get to the truth that will resolve the issue from within. This is the moment when you take the reins of control. You have moved your conscious awareness away from the upset part to the wise minister and healer governing your life destiny. From that place of power, you compassionately guide the Inner Aspect, that part of you that is feeling the emotional upset, through the seven steps to its complete resolution and healing.

Time is of the essence. It is best to do TheQuest Seven Steps within 24 to 48 hours of an upset, otherwise, the feelings recede and it is harder to identify and work with the part of you that is up for healing. You want to work with this part, because it has a direct relationship with the challenge you are facing.

The Inner Aspect will feel like a victim, but it has helped create the problem. It is the saboteur and the one that drew in the challenge. Its programming dictated its fate. And, you are there to free it.

In **Step Two**, you find how the subconscious aspect has been affecting you in each area of your life. It may be shutting you down or constricting you. It may be a volcano that explodes, ruining your core relationships and destroying your self-esteem. Whatever its affect on you mentally, emotionally, physically, and spiritually, whether it is creating an illness, undermining your health, destroying your peace of mind, or causing immense stress, allow it to share with you openly. If you judge it, the Inner Aspect will not only go away and hide from your conscious awareness, but the condition will remain unchanged. And the pattern will continue to create similar situations in your life until you are finally ready to deal with it.

In **Step Three**, you trace the history of the pattern back to the original wound. Let the Inner Aspect guide you through its painful past, reviewing the histories it brings to your conscious awareness. Keep your mind quiet. Don't try to remember the past or to think up the answers to the questions. Just relax and let the Inner Aspect show you.

You want to steadily guide it back to the originating incident. Following the history into the past is important for your Inner Aspect, because it allows it to see where its pattern stemmed from and how it was reinforced in your life. To make sure you have reached this originating point in time, ask the Inner Aspect if this is where it took on the pattern.

Think of this process as if you are lovingly taking the hand of someone who is very wounded and hurt. You are following them down into the caverns of the psyche to what could be a very dark and scary past for them. Your love, compassion and caring is the key. The Inner Aspect will trust you to know what is best and will allow you to guide it to its complete healing. This is its journey to freedom and the result for the Inner Aspect will be enlightenment and peace.

In **Step Four** you will discover the point in time when the Inner Aspect took on the beliefs and self-judgments that created the pattern. This is a very important step for the Inner Aspect because this is where it was imprinted with misinterpretations about itself. These self-judgments are usually something like, "I am unworthy of love. I don't matter. I am not good enough. Something is wrong with me. I am bad." The Inner Aspect may feel ruined, damaged, or stained. It will have influenced your life from this vantage point, permeating your conscious reality.

Core beliefs become patterns that are etched in time. These reoccurring patterns play movies that reinforce beliefs like "I am not good enough," and will continue until you go to the heart of the belief system and change it at its core.

You also pick up beliefs that are passed down through your family lineage by family members who are struggling with their own life conditions. These beliefs can be, "Life is hard. Suffering and pain are a part of life." Religious beliefs similarly traverse family lines such as, "I am a sinner that must pay for my sins." There is a host of beliefs and self-judgments that have plagued the human race and created suffering as a way of life on earth. We all have similar core beliefs, but the way we got them is our unique story.

Once the Inner Aspect has become aware of this imprint, you help it trace the effects forward to the present time, seeing how they influenced your life. You are now able to see the real reason for your life challenges. This is an elemental key to understanding life conditions and how they originate in the psyche, first as beliefs, and then reoccurring patterns. When this takes place in the session, there is an awakening that helps you see your responsibility in the equation. It is not that we consciously will "bad" things to happen to us, it's just that our core beliefs form patterns that create the challenges in our life. The good news is that once identified, these beliefs can be changed and the patterns healed. Once this takes place, the outer condition will shift.

I included Step Four in TheQuest Counseling technique because of its significance in bringing conscious awareness that on some level we do create our reality, and because it is our creation, not the will of an outer deity or accounting system, we can change it. When you fully understand that the reoccurring patterns in your life are born from these beliefs and how they have adversely affected your life, you hold an important key to your freedom.

Once your Inner Aspect is fully aware of how your inner programming was being reflected in your outer reality, you gently guide it back to the originating incident to see what the real truth is.

This is when Self Forgiveness can work wonders. Place your hand on your heart, the other on your stomach. Repeat the following until you feel clear. "I forgive myself for judgming myself as...." or, "I forgive myself for buying into the belief that I am....".

Finally, have the Inner Aspect see what is really true. Are the beliefs and self-judgments it took on accurate? The Inner Aspect will find that it is innately pure, not bad or evil at its core. It is lovable, it is good enough, it is worthy of love.

This is when a powerful inner shift occurs. You have gone down into the core wounding and are now emerging with the Truth. The part of you that was stamped with this pattern and scarred from the painful life experiences, is now free to fulfill its highest potential. Though it may have felt ruined, tainted, or destroyed, it will be released from the fate dictated by the programming. In that moment, a complete history is being laid to rest and a new future is beginning to dawn on your horizon.

It is in **Step Five** that you gain an overview of why the pattern served you and what the Inner Aspect wanted to accomplish. This helps you to understand the greater purpose behind the challenges you faced and how they were important for your life. This is a powerful step that takes victimhood out of the equation, because it frees you from the sense that you are a victim to your fate. You begin to see the perfection in everything you've gone through and why it was important for you. You are uncovering the truth, overcoming the pattern, and freeing yourself from false beliefs that created a false identity. As the cause of your pain is healed, the pattern will no longer be playing out in your future. You will be free!

Your subconscious patterns provide life circumstances that challenge you in unique ways, and each serves you in accomplishing something important. You may have become stronger, you may have more insights into human nature, or you may have greater compassion and desire to help others. They help forge your destiny and assist you in finding your True Purpose.

Once you see how the pattern served you and what gifts you gained from it, your Inner Aspect will feel complete. It will now be ready to let go of the pattern and be a positive, rather than challenging, support in your life. The Inner Aspect will no longer need the pattern to fulfill its goal in challenging you for your own betterment.

In **Step Six**, you ask your Inner Aspect to give you a new image of the new intention it has for you. You have it place the new image next to the old one, so you can see the difference. The new one will be radiant, powerful and strong, while the old one will be wearing the affliction it was overcome with.

In **Step Seven**, when your Inner Aspect is ready, you have it step into and merge with the new image, bringing all the wisdom, learning, and growth it gained, and letting go of all detrimental aspects of the pattern, including the pain, self judgments, and beliefs it took on. In that moment, a powerful inner transformation takes place. The Inner Aspect is now free, enlightened, and clear. You have transformed the shadow to light, your upset to peace, your pain to joy, and restored a flawed facet of your personality to its innate design. This Sacred Alchemy of the Soul is a deep inner process that alchemically changes the very nature of your life experience. It undoes the past and transforms the future. It restores you to your True Self, the part of you that is always in peace.

With this understanding of the subconscious and the knowledge that you can skillfully heal and transform every challenge in your life, you no longer need to live with painful dynamics or feel burdened about your past. You can step free from memories that have plagued you. By healing your patterns, the conditions of your life give way to allow a more enlightened, harmonious, and fulfilling existence. The Truth of who you are shines through! The baggage you've carried for so long is gone! Jewels of Wisdom have replaced painful histories as your past is reframed. You understand and are at peace.

Share Your Experience: I'd love to hear about your experience with TheQuest and to receive testimonials for this work if you feel it has benefited you. You can Email your experience, testimonial, or personal story to me at: Info@AEOS.ws

CHAPTER FIVE

Creating Time for Your Healing

One of the essential elements in TheQuest Life Mastery Path is to create time and space for your healing. This is time for you. Make it special.

Create a Safe Space: When giving yourself a counseling session, it is important to first prepare a space where you will feel comfortable. Turn off the phones and make sure you will be left undisturbed. Lighting a candle, burning incense, creating a centerpiece with flowers or healing stones can be very comforting. Add your own special touch to create the atmosphere most inspiring to you. You can find a serene nature setting, sit in a beautiful garden, or do your Self Counseling at the beach. Get creative! This is a powerful experience and one that can be deeply empowering and restoring.

TheQuest Self Counseling Journal: Journaling your process can be empowering. It allows you to trace the history of your Self Counseling sessions and see where and when you addressed and healed a pattern. You begin to see how powerful this work is in changing your life circumstances and altering your future. The more creatively you express in your journal, the more you will be inspired to bring your issues there.

This is Sacred Time: A time to express yourself fully and to heal parts of you that were wounded in the past. This Self Counseling process is nurturing to the wounded spirit, allowing the deepest reflections to take place. It can restore you quickly and help you come through the most challenging experiences unscathed.

Centering: Centering yourself and then beginning with a clear intention or prayer for the session is very powerful. You can ask that the greatest healing take place within the deepest levels of your psyche, your family line, and in humanity, being specific about the upset or pattern you want to resolve.

TheQuest Self Counseling Technique: You will find TheQuest Seven Steps in the next chapter. Simply follow each step until your Inner Aspect is completely healed and transformed. To do this, you must first get in touch with your emotions. Once you have done that, you can step back into a neutral observer position to work with the part of you that is upset. The key is to get a clear visual image of the Inner Aspect during Step One. Once you are able to identify the upset aspect, you can then take it through the Seven Steps.

It is important to be kind and compassionate with the Inner Aspect rather than judgmental. Criticism of your feelings and the part of you that is upset will only drive it away from your conscious awareness. If that happens, you won't be able to work with it. Not feeling safe, it will recede back into your psyche until a future time when it is triggered again. Meanwhile, the pattern it is holding will continue to bring dysfunctional relationships and challenging situations into your life.

Think of the Inner Aspect as a child who needs your care and attention, even though it may appear in adult form. Many Inner Aspects received their encoding in childhood, but they may appear older when you begin working with them.

You want to heal each troubled aspect of your psyche as it comes into your conscious awareness because it is the one holding the code to the subconscious programming that is responsible for your outer challenge. To unlock this code and reprogram it, you must work on it directly in the subconscious where the patterning occurred.

Where to Begin: At the top of your journal page, write the date so that you can trace your positive life changes and victories to the specific session and pattern you healed. Then begin with Step One, writing, "1. Identification." Follow the instructions, writing out the answers and continue this format throughout the counseling session. Feel free to draw your aspect as it goes through the different changes during your session.

Remember:

Emotions are your allies. They appear at the perfect time to lead you into the psyche where you will find the next pattern ready to be healed.

- Always treat yourself and your Inner Aspects with love and respect.

- The more compassionately you embrace an Inner Aspect, the more willing it is to share its story with you. This will help you to traverse the dark regions of the psyche, bringing healing to even the most challenging aspects.

- If you ever feel stuck, or the aspect is not responding, go back to the previous question and continue working with it until all the important information is gathered and it feels good about going to the next step.

Once you become proficient in this work, you will be able to do the Seven Steps effortlessly as issues arise. Addressing your issues and healing your inner patterns will become second nature.

CHAPTER SIX

TheQuest Seven Steps

When you apply TheQuest Self Counseling Technique, you are working on a deep unconscious level. The inner shift you will undergo will then ripple out to positively affect your life. This can bring miraculous results to challenges that have felt unchangeable or insurmountable. Remember, every issue can be resolved and every pattern healed. You can change the conditions of your life!

You may want to try TheQuest Self Counseling now or skip over this chapter and come back when you feel ready to experience the powerful healing it provides. Remember, leaving your issues unaddressed or ignoring your feelings can have detrimental effects. Doing your Self Counseling in a timely way can bring immediate relief and give you the ability to more effectively handle what you are facing in your life.

Step One: Identification

1. Review what you're going through, or a condition or illness you are facing, and what you are feeling. Allow yourself to feel your feelings fully, then write these feelings down.

2. Next, move back into your Authentic Self, so that you can get a clear visual image of the part of you that is feeling this way and that has the condition, giving it loving attention rather than criticism or judgment. Visual imaging is important. *Once you can see an Inner Aspect, you can heal it.*

3. Draw a picture of your Inner Aspect and then write down everything it is feeling. If the upset is a result of what happened with another individual, you can draw them as well, so you can get a clear visual image of this dynamic.

An Important Key: Your dynamics with others are a reflection of what is happening inside of you. The sooner you move your attention away from what is going on between you and the other person, the quicker you will resolve your issues and be able to effectively deal with the situation.

Application: The two images you see described on the page are no longer you and the other person. They now represent your own Inner Aspects. Because they have gotten your attention, they are now ready to be healed. In this way, the other person's unconscious words or actions supported you by triggering a deep pattern or wound that is ready for healing.

If you are dealing with an illness, financial constraint, or other challenging situation, include that in the image, showing how the Inner Aspect is being adversely affected.

Step Two: Influence

Now it is time to begin working directly with your Inner Aspect. Ask the Inner Aspect how it has been affecting you on all levels (physically, mentally, emotionally, spiritually) and how it has been influencing your life (relationships, health, career, finances.) Write down each level and the answers. (MENTAL, EMOTIONAL, PHYSICAL, SPIRITUAL, HEALTH, CAREER, FINANCES, RELATIONSHIPS)

Step Three: History

Ask the Inner Aspect to show you the history of similar feelings and experiences all the way back to where the pattern originated and then see what was taking place at that earliest time. Make sure you are at the earliest time and write the highlights.

Step Four: The Truth

1. Find the self-judgment and core beliefs it took on from that earliest experience. (I was unloved, therefore I am unlovable. I'm not wanted, I don't matter, I'm not good enough, etc.)

2. See how these judgments and beliefs influenced your life, tracing the pattern forward to the present time.

3. Go back to the original incident and see if the judgments and beliefs were really true. It helps to go over what was really happening. Ask the Inner Aspect to update each judgment and belief with the new realization.

4. Next, Self Forgiveness can be a powerful healing salve. Place one hand on your heart, the other on your stomach and say, "I forgive myself for judging myself as (or, I forgive myself for believing...)" going through all the judgments and then stating the Truth.

Step Five: The Gift

1. Ask the Aspect, "Why was this pattern and the experiences it created important for me? What was the gift? What did you want to accomplish?" The Inner Aspect provided you with a 'vehicle of experience.' Have the Inner Aspect review and see what you gained from the pattern. What was the learning and growth?

2. Once you have received a positive answer, ask, "Do you feel you have accomplished that?" If the answer is no, take the Inner Aspect back through some of the previous questions until it has accessed everything it needs to move on.

3. Ask the Inner Aspect, "Do you feel complete with the pattern?" The answer should be yes.

4. Then ask, "What would my future look like if you chose to continue the pattern instead?" Remember to keep writing the answers in your journal, stopping to tune in to your Inner Aspect as you go along.

Step Six: New Purpose

The Inner Aspect should now be ready to support you in a higher way. Ask the Inner Aspect how it will serve you now, and ask it to give you a new visual image of what that would look like, placing the new image beside the original one. Draw or describe this new image in your journal, listing it's New Purpose.

Step Seven: Transfiguration

1. When it is ready, have the Aspect merge with the new image, retaining all the learning, growth, wisdom, and knowledge it gained, while dissolving all aspects of the pattern that no longer are serving you. This should include all the anger, upset, and pain it was feeling and all the self-judgments it was holding.

2. Once complete, ask "How will my life be different now that you've been healed and transformed?" Draw or describe the transfigured Aspect.

3. Ask the Transformed Aspect, "What action steps should I take to support this session?" Write those down. Having a copy of them will remind you, so you can stay on track with supporting the inner shift that has occurred.

Integration: You have just gone through a very deep and powerful inner process. Allow yourself time to anchor the new information. You may want to do some additional writing, listen to inspiring music, or just have some time alone in nature. This quiet time is important for you to integrate what you have been through. It will allow you to more fully understand the pattern you healed and what it created in your life. You can emerge from this process with a new sense of empowerment and compassion for yourself and others. Remember to journal your experience and make notes relating to your session when your life changes in the future.

Congratulations! You have now successfully completed your first Self Counseling Session. Remember to use the Seven Steps whenever you feel upset or are facing a challenging life situation. Use this counseling technique before you work on issues with your mate, colleague, child, or friend. You'll be a lot clearer and more able to come from a centered, compassionate place, where you will be able to listen as well as share your experience in a loving way.

Feel free to share TheQuest with loved ones and friends. The more people that adopt Self Counseling as a part of their lifestyle, the more a true and lasting change in relationships can occur, positively affecting the consciousness of the planet. With such a dramatic shift away from victimhood and blame, the world can transform very quickly, allowing peace to replace suffering as a way of life.

CHAPTER SEVEN

The Doctrine of Pain

You may believe it is not possible to find inner peace, or you may have been taught that challenges are a part of life. Suffering is a part of human existence, something that you must accept and endure. Even our most revered religious documents speak of suffering as a way of life.

This doctrine of pain has been reinforced over time by a host of saints, sages, and holy persons. Hell fire and damnation sermons continue from the pulpits to this day, as well-meaning ministers pass this belief to their congregations. Parents attending these sermons pass it on to their children, until most people have been programmed to believe there is no escape.

In the Catholic Tradition, the Stations of the Cross symbolize not only the places Jesus fell under the weight of his personal trials, but also the path that every sincere applicant for God's Grace should take. Good Christians are inspired to "pick up your cross and follow Jesus," and to abstain from joyful activities that are contrary to this doctrine of suffering. No wonder many people feel guilty when they experience pleasure. Pleasure and happiness have been toted as the way of the devil, while hardship, challenges, setbacks, and pain as the way to please God.

Countless individuals today believe they need to be crucified to be worthy of God's love. They are imperfect sinners who must be cleansed of their sins and suffering is the way. The more they suffer, the happier God is with them. We see this in the martyr pattern that is so prevalent on earth. Many people are living in the direst circumstances, many accepting abuse as their lot in life. They endure the worst treatment because deep inside they believe they are unworthy of love. They are carrying an unconscious shame that is beneath their everyday awareness and yet it is so strong that it is dictating their way of life.

You speak to these people about their experiences and find they are resigned to their fate. They married the person and now must make the best of it. They've made their bed and now must lie in it. These prevalent beliefs in the psyche of humanity must be cleared before we can see a shift in world conditions. Individuals worldwide must wake up to the fact that their subconscious beliefs are dictating the future of our planet. If we continue to hold onto false beliefs, convinced that we are unworthy of anything more, we will continue to reap the same results. We will perpetuate suffering and this will continue down our family lines until the world reflects a prison colony rather than a golden age.

We must lay to rest the myths of the past and adopt a new attitude based on the fact that we are worthy, we are lovable, we are precious, and we do matter. We must cast out old notions that God is mean, fierce, and unforgiving, and realize that Love is the True Divine Nature and this Love brings understanding, compassion and forgiveness. If we build our world upon these principles, it will look very different from the current theme of "an eye for an eye," enmity, intolerance, and hate.

To truly forgive we must look deeper to find out why others behave as they do. With the knowledge of subconscious patterns and how they are passed from generation to generation and rule people's lives, you can more clearly comprehend the challenges others go through. You can have more patience with their human failings, and you can forgive even the worst behaviors.

Compassionate understanding of others and ourselves allows us to truly know what Love is about. It is then we are embodying our highest nature, the part of us that is always connected with the Divine and which lives forever in a transcendent reality that fosters peace and understanding.

The Shadow will never comprehend this level of maturity and wisdom until it is fully healed, for it clings to its version of victimhood, always making others wrong for its experience. It lives out of its wound and this permeates our conscious reality until we believe as it believes and we live as it dictates rather than from our Authentic Self. As we cast off old beliefs held sacred by Shadow Aspects, we come more fully into an empowered maturity, and our life shifts accordingly. We view things from a clearer perspective and are free from superstitions and myths that have cast souls into darkness throughout time.

As the Shadow is healed, we have clearer boundaries and can

experience more conscious relationships. When we know we are worthy, we create lives that reflect our self-esteem. We feel supported from within and so our path becomes less arduous. We stand for what is our highest good and live an exemplary life. It is then we build our foundation upon the Principles of Peace.

Part Three

TheQuest
7 Master Keys to Inner Peace

TheQuest Master Keys

The seven basic principles of TheQuest are Master Keys to Actualize your Full Potential and attain Inner Peace. When applied, you are no longer a victim to your fate, nor are you susceptible to the victim consciousness so prevalent in humanity today. You take responsibility for your life and you take command of every situation in a masterful way.

The Seven Master Keys are…

1. Take Back Your Power
2. You Are Not Your Patterns
3. Eliminate the Virus In Your Human Computer
4. Walk Your Highest Destiny Path
5. There is No True Victimhood
6. Challenging People Serve You
7. Suffering is Not the Will of God

THE FIRST MASTER KEY

Take Back Your Power

The subconscious wields more power in the physical world than you might imagine. Its programs physically shape matter and create challenging circumstances no matter what you are thinking, feeling, intending, or believing. Not even God can change the circumstances of your life if your subconscious is not willing. That is why humanity is reaping so much less than the Eden of Earth's beginning. Subconscious patterns have taken hold and literally ruined the planet.

All adverse situations can be traced to programs running in your subconscious. These include relational issues, physical conditions, illnesses, addictions, and financial constraint. These patterns permeate your personality and often run beneath your conscious awareness. That is why others can see them many times when you cannot. They make up the Shadow Self that is continually driving you with its unconscious fears and desires. This Shadow Self overruns your consciousness with upsets and distress. You set clear intentions and it sabotages them. You affirm positive ideals and yet, many times manifest so much less.

Your Authentic or Core Self is very different. It illumines you with wisdom, empowers you with strength. It has a commanding presence. It is powerful yet compassionate, clear and directed, peaceful and relaxed. It is the highest, best of you, and it is always present within you no matter what your Conscious Self is focused on. But most people are out of touch with their Authentic Self and live life from the fate dictated by Shadow (or subconscious) patterns.

You have to consciously take back the power from your Shadow Self or it will keep ruining your life. To become its master, (the master of your psychology), you must refuse to let the Shadow run you. The moment it arises, you must take command and move into action to address and heal it.

Every life challenge is caused by these patterns. It is your subconscious wielding its power in your physical world. The more quickly you address your situation on the subconscious level, the faster you will move through it and the less time you will spend suffering.

TheQuest Seven Steps provide the way for you to quickly heal a Shadow Aspect the moment it begins playing out in your world. By quelling the shadow appearances, you empower your Authentic Self and begin to embody your True Nature.

Each inner pattern dictating hardship must be changed. Wherever you are being limited, held back, harmed, or blocked, you will have a sabotaging subconscious pattern running. Each outer condition has a corresponding inner pattern. Each pattern may be held in place by one or more subconscious personalities that have been wired through false beliefs to run a false program. Each pattern is a virus in the human psyche that has corrupted the human computer and it is very powerful in its ability to override your True Nature.

A virus will continue to raise havoc in your world until it is eliminated and Inner Aspects that have been corrupted by the virus will continue to run the same pattern until they are reprogrammed. It is a simple equation. Placing positive affirming information into the computer may have a beneficial overall effect on you mentally, but it will not alter your subconscious programs or the deeper anxiety permeating your life. You must deal with patterns directly in the subconscious to create a change.

Once you understand how the subconscious works, you move into action quickly when challenges arise. You know there is a deeper place that must be addressed and you get right to it. It is then the patterns creating the havoc are changed and your life is transformed.

THE SECOND MASTER KEY

You Are Not Your Patterns

You may have become so enmeshed in your subconscious programming that you feel out of touch with the peace of your True Nature. You strive for a better life, but fall victim to horrible fates. You long to be content, but struggle through endlessly trying circumstances until you become lost in a miasm of personality fluctuations. These fluctuations may have you feeling strong in one moment and then weak or insecure in the next. You are clear, directed, and confident, and then, overwhelmed or confused. It is in rare moments, if any, you are able to sustain the equanimity of your Authentic Self. Subconscious patterns continually get in the way.

Because you have not known who you really are, you identify with the part of you that is having the emotional response. You think you are the one that is upset rather than understanding that there is a part of you that is upset. You feel envious, jealous and insecure and believe you are that way, that it is part of your True Nature. So you stay locked in your emotional responses to life, a victim to subconscious sub-personalities, never realizing you are so much more.

The truth is, you are powerful. You are talented. You have a unique gift to share. You are needed. You are important to our planetary equation, but you've forgotten who you are. You are under the amnesia inherent on this planet and so you believe you are your dysfunctional personality traits. Labeling yourself with titles like, "I'm a workaholic. I'm lazy. I'm a controller. I'm a procrastinator," your True Self remains lost from view.

You may even have identified with your Shadow to such a degree that you've failed to see what lies behind the illusion of your Shadow Nature. Stress and strain may have become such a normal way of life that it is only in rare moments that you settle down into yourself and feel the peace of your True Nature. That is when everything in the world feels right. That is when everything becomes clear. That is when you command your life from a clear, calm center.

When you strive to overcome your challenges by an outer means, ignoring the inner component, subconscious patterns will continue to sabotage you. Becoming physical realities of a challenging nature, they will block the greater good from manifesting in your life, leaving you in a destitute wilderness. Left unaddressed, they will never change. Suffering will continue as a way of life and you will continue to be a victim to your subconscious fate.

Applying Step One in TheQuest Self Counseling the moment you are overcome by an upset emotion, you can break free in minutes and have your Authentic Self back in the driver's seat. It really is not hard to live this masterful life.

An inner physics must be applied if humanity is going to end suffering on earth. No outer means will change the endless dramas and the escalation of planetary problems unless the root cause is addressed and the programming responsible is changed. This is something we must each take responsibility for and it is this level of work that could be our best offering to a world in travail. If humanity understood this one powerful equation we could change the world.

THE THIRD MASTER KEY

Eliminate the Virus in Your Human Computer

Humanity has forever struggled with serious conditions, believing that challenge and suffering is a way of life. Trapped in never-ending troubles, the people in this world have not known how to change the challenging circumstances in their lives. Feeling like victims, they resign themselves to their lot in life or wear themselves out trying to change a seemingly inescapable destiny. A virus has gotten into the human computer and it has reprogrammed our planet into a world of strife.

If you've ever felt trapped in a situation that felt like a prison, you will know what it feels like for a majority of people on the planet. They work harder and faster to dig themselves out of trouble, but no matter how hard they try, they can't escape. The walls of the prison close in around them so securely, they can feel the cold steel bars in their hands.

They may pound their fists on the prison walls. They may cry out for God to release them. They may shudder at the thought of being relegated to a life sentence and in their heart of hearts, long for freedom and peace, but there's no way out. No amount of prayer, affirmations, or creative visualizations makes a dent. They remain held in the grip of financial constraint, a serious illness, an overweight condition, addiction, or challenging relationship dynamic. They are continually upset, strained and stressed. Their life circumstance feels like a prison sentence, incurable and unchangeable. Finally they let go and submit to their fate. They turn to the bottle, get lost in television, overeat, or sit in denial that anything is wrong.

Such was the case with a talented man who had become entrenched in a romantic alliance that felt like a prison. While he continually strove to escape, life circumstances rendered him powerless to move on. When asked if he had addressed the subconscious patterns in charge of his situation, he simply said, "I'm doing my daily affirmations and visualizations." Meanwhile, years were passing by.

It is a rare individual who understands the power of the subconscious and has the tools to extricate their self from the past and create a new future. A majority of people just submit themselves to their fate. They give up when the going gets tough and learn to live with their challenges, believing that is all they deserve. They wear the burkas of disempowerment. They take abuse from their mates. They live with ridicule and judgment. They dream of an abundant life while accepting minimum wage jobs that barely meet their family's needs, failing to get the education, training, or job experience that would give them a better life. They kill themselves to achieve their goals while barely enjoying the precious time they are allotted on earth.

The future becomes all-important while the present is laid to waste. Finally, the dreams that once lit up their eyes become dying embers as they resort to what they've been taught, "Life is hard. This is your karma. You must submit to your fate. That is how it is on earth."

So many beliefs have left humanity cut off from the power of the Authentic Self and their rightful inheritance. These beliefs become patterns etched in time. Anchored in the subconscious, they play out in the physical world, perpetuating strife until the dream of a better future is erased from the minds of the people.

Most of us know people who are stuck in circumstances or who keep revolving the same life pattern. We see this with the abused woman who continually manifests the next abusive mate, the henpecked, dominated man who continually does his wife's bidding, or the alcoholic whose life revolves around drinking. We want to help them extricate themselves from their troubles. We may spend endless hours counseling them or even showing them a way out, but they remain rooted in their problems, or keep manifesting the same fate.

Perhaps you have felt trapped in a relationship, life drama, challenging circumstance, or illness. To change this woeful inheritance, the inner virus must be addressed. This is powerful magic and a lost secret that has been buried in time. When you understand that every painful condition was first a pattern in your subconscious, you can unweave the viruses in your human computer and change the circumstances of your life.

THE FOURTH MASTER KEY

Walk Your Highest Destiny Path

To manifest a higher vision for your life, you must remove the inner blocks that are in place. To have the loving relationship you seek, you must heal the inner dynamic causing your distress. To change your financial situation, you need to change the subconscious programming that has caused the condition. Because your outer circumstances have a direct relationship to these inner programs, they are easy to trace. Just follow your upset emotions to their source.

When you apply TheQuest Seven Steps to each challenging condition, you unlock the door of the prison, and bring an end to what could have been a life sentence. When you heal your patterns, your life circumstances are transformed in the twinkling of an eye. In that moment, you have changed your future. You have altered your destiny by stepping onto a future line that is free of the patterns you've released. This activates another destiny potential, perhaps beyond what you would have previously imagined for yourself, one where the Authentic Self is more able to dictate the journey, now that you are free of the subconscious patterning. This is how you can walk your highest destiny path, fulfill your Divine Plan, and enjoy a life of greater fulfillment.

TheQuest Life Mastery Path is designed to lead you out of the wilderness of your shadow awareness to the empowered life of your Authentic Self. It is a light at the end of the tunnel of your present challenges, a way out of the darkness, and a return to peace. It is a way to end strife so that you can realize your greater potential.

The only way to fulfill your potential, is to stop being run by your Shadow. When you take command of your psychology and stop living in the grip of subconscious patterns, you become a Master of Your Life. That is when you can fulfill a higher destiny.

THE FIFTH MASTER KEY

There Is No True Victimhood

Contrary to popular planetary belief, there is no true victimhood. Victimhood is a misconception, a misinterpretation of events. While many situations seem like there are victims and we hear victim stories every day from our family and friends, in thousands of sessions I have never once found a case where someone was really the victim. Let me explain.

When you are maligned, wronged, harmed, or something precious of yours is destroyed, subconscious personalities are at work. They are powerful magnets drawing all the challenging circumstances into your life. Many times this is an attempt to resolve past issues or to fulfill needs that are unmet.

The true cause behind every life challenge lies within. Even in countless sessions uncovering the severest histories of violence and abuse, I have consistently found a place of responsibility in the subconscious. The awareness that on this deep level we are creating our reality and that the worst people in our lives are in fact serving our unconscious patterns, cured me of any belief in victimhood.

This doesn't mean that we don't feel victimized when catastrophes happen or losses occur. We all go through experiences that hurt us. We are taken advantage of, people abuse us, and false accusations sting us. At these times, our conscious self naturally feels like a victim and our supporting cast of social conscience in friends and family believes we are victims and that victimhood prevails on earth. But victims have no power to change the circumstances in their lives. They are weakened by their belief in random acts without meaning or a fate that is delivered without warning by an outside force. They are burdened with the idea that life is unfair, that the trials people endure in the world are unjust, or that they are being punished. It is only when people trace their life conditions to patterns within their subconscious that they are able to see where they are responsible for what they are creating in their lives and then can change them.

None of us consciously chooses to have painful experiences. We are not thinking, "I would like to marry an abuser," or "I want to struggle with an addiction," or "I think it would be good for me to have immense financial challenges." We are not masochists willing bad things to happen to us, but we do have subconscious patterns that are creating situations that cause us to suffer and that make life hard to endure. To change that in ourselves and in our world, we have to go into the subconscious body and make the changes there.

If you trace the adversity in your life history you will find the good that came from your personal challenges. It is exciting to uncover the truth behind these difficult experiences. When clients come to this point in the session, it is so freeing. Finally, there is an answer, an understanding that you didn't have before and with that comes a sense of rightness and peace. Even though you may have been severely challenged, had your heart broken, lost valuable possessions, or had something taken that meant everything to you, if you trace these events to the deepest levels and see the inner strengths these situations inspired, you will realize that there was a greater purpose behind your suffering and that even the worst conditions brought with them learning and growth.

We need to stop commiserating with the people around us and understand that the victim story is inaccurate. It stems from an irrational viewpoint that does not understand that there's a level of responsibility for everything that is taking place in our outer reality.

When we see how our shadowed aspects have created the problems in our life, then we are in a position of power to change them. We can repair the flaws in our nature and empower ourselves in the physical universe. This is what true empowerment means. We need to empower the people in our lives to look deeper so they can take responsibility for their reactions and what is happening in their life. This deep inquiry will allow them to get to the heart of what is really going on for them, why they are triggered, what got activated, what self-esteem issues, core belief system, and wound is calling to be healed?

We need to understand that this is a victorious pathway,

that our life is about empowerment on every level and restoring the facets of our Diamond Nature. It is not about progressing the disempowerment story. It is time that we pass a legacy of truth to our children and stop passing on this misinterpretation any longer. It is time we restore the facets of our divine nature and stop living out of the limited human reality that keeps us at 10% of our potential. We must accept the Truth about our lives and what is happening to us. The only way we can do this is by paying attention to our emotional responses to life and the victim parts that are calling to us from our psyche.

While traversing the many challenges of this Earth Schoolroom, you can learn to use everything to your advancement and to create blessings from even the worst circumstances. This is called making lemonade out of the lemons you are handed in life, a gift TheQuest Self Counseling provides. Each experience is an opportunity for soul advancement and no matter how devastating or painful the situation, you can emerge victorious.

Challenges are a blessing. They are opportunities for great growth, learning and advancement. Without challenges, you would never get in touch with your patterns or heal them. You would not be able to rise to ever-new levels of soul awareness through overcoming obstacles and emerging victorious over your life circumstances.

Finding the purpose behind your life challenges is one of the most rewarding aspects of TheQuest Life Mastery Path. When you know that life is supporting you on an incredible journey, you cease to be a victim and you become free of the victim consciousness. You emerge from each challenge empowered, and you feel victorious.

THE SIXTH MASTER KEY

Challenging People Serve You

The most challenging people in your life give you the greatest movement and growth. Playing a challenging role for you not only serves the dictates of your inner programming, it assists you in your soul advancement. No matter how horrible, unconscious or cruel they are, there is an important service rendered.

The way this works is a secret alchemy. Their words, actions, or behaviors will trigger an emotional response in you. This will lead you to the pattern that created the situation in the first place. By healing the pattern, you step free of the challenging relationship dynamic, because the person will no longer need to serve you in this way.

When you find yourself in a challenging situation with someone, it is a reflection of two Inner Aspects that are in conflict within you. The key is to step back from the outer situation while you tend to the inner, because the easiest way to change the dynamic is by taking care of your part. By doing the Inner Work, you emerge feeling empowered and clear with another facet of your Shadow Self healed and transformed.

When you clear your piece, it allows the other person the opportunity to make positive changes and shift the way in which they are relating to you. This is how the person's unconscious behavior can serve you, which is a completely different way of looking at relationship challenges than the victim point of view so prevalent on the planet.

It is sometimes only through these outer dynamics that you can see what is going on inside of you. Like an ever-ascending stairway to personal empowerment, relationship issues serve you by drawing your attention to what personality flaw needs to be worked on next. An initiatic rite, each challenge provides the next step towards self-actualization. Traversing these steps helps you gain self-mastery. As you ascend each step, a resolution takes place and your inner peace is restored.

THE SEVENTH MASTER KEY

Suffering is Not the Will of God

One of the most important discoveries I've made is that there is no outer deity dictating our fate. No one is willing suffering upon us, neither are challenging circumstances a curse to punish humanity. I know this is contrary to many religious beliefs, but I never once found God behind someone's challenge in any session. What I did find is that we punish ourselves.

I know that's a lot to swallow, but this self-infliction is not from a conscious desire or intention, it is our subconscious that is willing these things in motion. I found in every case covering every hardship, lack, and challenge imaginable, that subconscious patterns were behind it. Tracing each condition to its root cause, I found sub-personalities in charge each time. While this was shocking because of my own beliefs, it is actually good news, because that means we can change the conditions in our lives. We are not relegated to a horrible fate with no escape. We can heal the sub-personalities in charge of our life challenges. We don't need to continually suffer for our mistakes (sins). We can heal our lives, forgive our past, and move on to a better future.

I also found an Indwelling Presence at the core of each person's being, beyond the sub-personalities creating havoc in their lives. This innate personality was consistently holding a powerful intention for their lives. It wanted them to be happy, prosperous, and at peace, and had compassion for their plight.

Just as a flower blossoms from a seed encoded with its true nature, and a tree grows strong and tall from a tiny acorn, so it is with each soul who embodies on earth. Each child was born into this world in the innocence and purity of its True Nature and each carries within them a secret code that if allowed, will in time fulfill a unique destiny.

We were born to a greater glory, but we have been stamped with a human programming that moved us away from our innate innocence. And yet, no matter how dominant the Shadow Self has become, there is an Indwelling Presence that lives on within us, ever guiding us to the greater good.

We are not and never were sinners that deserve to suffer. We are more like wayward children who have forgotten our lost heritage. We have become imbedded in a programming that has distorted our reality to the point where we long for peace but perpetuate suffering. This has taught us as nothing else could. Our direct experience with the dark side of our nature has illuminated the brilliance of our authentic selfhood. When we find it, it's like a bastion of hope shining forth in a dark night. It leads us through a purification where we are redeemed, until at last we are restored to our innate divinity.

We must be gentle with ourselves and forgive our wayward nature. Each mistake we make provides us with an opportunity to learn and grow and expand our conscious awareness, and ultimately this leads to our being more loving, compassionate and kind.

Often we learn our best lessons the hard way, and this is through making mistakes. This does not mean we are bad and deserve to suffer. It is just the nature of this world. We come in and go under an amnesia that many times includes the wisdom that would keep us out of trouble. We are like children going through the same life lessons over and over again, so that we can finally grow up and be our mature selves.

I've seen the best people go through the worst circumstances and for a long time, I could never understand why. Was life that unfair? Is earth a penal system where sinners come to suffer, only they can't remember what they did wrong? Is it true that if you are good you will suffer the worst treatment, because that is what saints must endure? No!

I searched to find the truth about these things, but found a different reality. The wounds we've gathered from our painful experiences create patterns that then continue until we heal them. That is why good people have "bad' things happen to them and why even the most conscious person can have reoccurring situations that cause suffering and pain.

Our challenges are really not about how positive, nice or

enlightened we are because challenges are not necessarily a result of how we are acting and behaving, but are born of patterns running in our subconscious. Our actions and behaviors are a result of this programming and yes, they can cause havoc but they are not the root cause.

Humans have fostered beliefs of a God that acts more like a monster. It is human doctrines that created a hell where people with incorrect religious beliefs go, including innocent babies and indigenous cultures cut off from the outer world. It is humans that refuse to forgive or have a compassionate understanding of one another, and we've projected this way of being onto God.

As I studied our present planetary situation from an inner perspective and worked directly in the psyche through a host of clients, I was brought each time to the heart of suffering. Applying my counseling technique, I watched these conditions transform. No God or devil was standing by willing the dark fate upon my client. Rather, there was a loving, forgiving, and deeply compassionate presence in every session.

I learned that the Universe is built upon loving principles and that within humanity and even in the worst people, there is an authentic selfhood that is reflective of a divine presence that must surely exist, because it is encoded within humanity.

It is time to raise the standard on Earth by embodying our innate divinity and allowing this Indwelling Light to shine. As we heal ourselves of the religious myths and subconscious programs that have perpetuated suffering, we will erase their reflection from our world.

Our journey through this crucial time inspires this level of commitment. It compels us to go deep into our psyche and to heal the collective patterns that are making devastating appearances across the globe. Each drama played out on earth represents a subconscious pattern in the psyche of humanity that is ready to be healed. Viewed from this perspective, doing our own inner healing work can greatly affect the present planetary equation. It can take the energy out of huge confrontations and devastating conditions, healing them quickly from within.

It is said our planet was once a Garden of Eden, but serpentine patterns set in and a new reality was set in motion that has traversed generations of time.

We believe in victimhood because we have lost touch with our ancient heritage and forfeited our divine birthright to live in harmony and peace.

We are not and never were victims to a divinely dictated fate, neither is there a powerful angry God smiting evildoers or bringing vengeance upon the wayward. We don't need to tremble in fear of God. We need to relax into the arms of the Divine Presence and the way to do that is to relax into the Indwelling Presence within us. That is the part of us that connects us to God and links us with every part of life everywhere. It is the part of us that knows there is a Benevolent Godlike Presence that skillfully guides the destiny of a universe of worlds, with a beneficent will for every part of life to prosper and blossom into its full potential.

Part Four

The Last Frontier

CHAPTER ONE

The Quest for Truth

It is time for us to take the next step in our human evolution, to go beyond the programming and conditioning that has created so much suffering in our world, and to live more conscious, joyous lives, finding the fulfillment that has for too long eluded us. And we can do it.

In the last century we saw the beginning of a great change as we ventured into the last frontier, the Inner World of the Soul. Seeking to understand the human dilemma and our purpose for being here, millions of people have begun to excavate the hidden regions of the psyche in a quest that is both empowering and life changing. Discontent with the limited knowledge available to fully understand our daily challenges, a grand search has begun that is taking us into a new era.

We are entering a time of conscious co-creation where we wake up to our responsibility to the planet and become wise stewards of our lives and of the earth. We are being called to address the human patterns that have limited our creative expression and kept us from accessing our full potential so that we can adequately address the challenges of our present planetary equation.

While many of us long for a better life, our everyday situations weigh heavily upon us. The endless round of financial struggles, personality conflicts, health issues and relationship dynamics keep our attention away from the grander purpose in life. We become immersed in the struggle and fail to comprehend the deeper meaning behind our existence.

Living under stress has become a way of life, while true happiness and inner peace continually elude us. We want to end suffering on the planet but we cannot seem to stop the misery of our own personal circumstances. Ever-new challenges continually arise, the strain increases, and we continue to live unfulfilled lives.

The discontent rumbling in the psyche of humanity is a catalyst for world change and this is happening inside of each one of us.

This discontent inspires a longing for something more, for that seemingly unattainable dream of peace and a sense of rightness about our life and reason for being here. That is when the inner quest begins.

In those moments of greatest struggle, when we are faced with surmounting difficulties, our soul cries out in anguish and pain so loudly we must take notice. The world, with its constant clamor for attention recedes and we turn our attention within.

What is this inner voice crying out for attention? What is the deep pain burning inside of me? Why do I continually reap misery in a world that is filled with such beauty and magnificence? Why the lack when there is so much abundance? Why so much suffering when I was originally patterned to joy?

As we move our awareness away from the outer world, a grand exploration begins. Listening to our emotions, we begin to tap into our feelings. Going further inside, we find a part of us that is hurting, calling out to us in pain. We begin to get an image of this part of us. "She is brokenhearted." "He is carrying a heavy burden." "She is hurt and angry."

These inner images make us curious to go beyond the barriers our lack of knowledge erected, into an inner world we've never traversed before because we have not known how to adequately deal with our emotional upheavals.

Religious doctrines have labeled them as bad and yet, no matter how good we try to be, in any given moment, we can change from happy to sad, content to miserable, loving to hateful, or from peace to rage no matter how strong our intentions are. And this has troubled us when prevalent doctrines on the planet tell us we are sinners and evil at our core.

As challenging conditions accelerate on the planet, we can no longer ignore the painful voices that arise from within. They are too strong. Virulent as hurricanes, they overwhelm our conscious awareness, holding us in a vise-like grip to the point where our shoulders are contracted and our stomachs become sick. We cannot function, we cannot think, and our decisions become fear-based as we are flung into a fight for survival.

We have not known how simple it is to effectively deal with this part of us or really what part it is. We have believed we are our emotions and that we had to keep our emotions locked inside where they can't do any harm. Meanwhile, they are eating us alive and making us ill. We want to medicate them away. We want to stay busy and keep ourselves distracted and yet, their voices of discontent echo through us like an eerie sound in the night and there is no escape!

When we ignore our inner voices, when we tune out the pain, when we saddle ourselves with endless activities, bury ourselves in overwork, or check out with alcohol or drugs, we deny ourselves access to the powerful part of us that holds our greater potential.

We remain ignorant, limited, deficient, or constrained. We stay in misery so much longer, waiting for someone or something outside of ourselves to change so we can be happy again. We long to realize our full potential, to live the life of our dreams. Instead we reap endless challenges and are unfulfilled in our personal lives.

When your life becomes challenging, when you face the darkest night, when you fall under the weight of personal circumstances, that is when your inner quest must begin. Powerful in its ability to relieve you of every burden, it also leads you to a lost treasure within.

CHAPTER TWO

Spiritual Bypass Is Making You Ill

While the world is filled with a rich spiritual heritage, the subconscious body has been left out of the equation. Unaddressed, it leaves us with a shadowed wilderland that continues to undermine our best efforts.

Through spiritual practices, we may enter high states of consciousness, become one with our True Nature, and through the experience, feel illumined and enlightened. We may believe we've reached that illustrious state attained by a few masters, and then within days, find ourselves feeling sad, angry, or hurt again. This has been a mystery that has baffled the most enlightened teachers, who in striving to set an exemplary example for their followers, can never quite stay in an "enlightened" state for long.

Contrary to planetary perception, enlightenment does not come with one touch from the guru's hand, freeing us for eternity from the patterns of our past. While seekers throughout the planet have flocked to ashrams and engaged in meditations, silent reflection, and the chanting of thousands of mantras, their subconscious patterns live on. This is because the subconscious body must be addressed directly, while affirmations and visualizations work largely on our mental body, shifting our consciousness. While the effect of these spiritual practices can be positive and uplifting, and help the aspirant to connect with their Authentic Self, understanding this difference is an important key to gaining self-mastery. It is only by addressing your subconscious patterns directly that you will be able to overcome your personality dysfunctions, patterns, and addictions.

Because most people have a hard time relating to personality afflictions, many tend to mentally or spiritually bypass their issues, rather than dealing with them. They disconnect from their feelings, move into positive thinking or a "spiritual consciousness," and believe that by not identifying with the problem it will disappear. They move away from the feelings that would put them in touch with the pattern creating their life challenge and so the pattern is never healed.

Many people try to magically transform their challenging situations by using affirmations or visualizations. Some even believe they can mentally will their life circumstances to change. However uplifted you keep your mental state, there is a powerful subconscious component that is often running below your conscious awareness and this should not be ignored. Positive imaging helps you have a clear direction in life, and positive thinking is beneficial to mental health, but if you coerce yourself into "being positive" while ignoring how you really feel, you can get ill.

Many people religiously avoid upset, anger, sadness, or fear because these emotions have been labeled as bad. This superstition is so prevalent in religious and spiritual communities that people feel they are committing a sin if they feel this way. "Bad things will happen to them. Negative thinking will draw in negative circumstances."

What people fail to realize is where negative thinking comes from. It is always a sub-personality that is thinking this way. If you simply change the channel, you disregard an important subconscious component. Dwelling in negative emotions is unhealthy, and negativity itself can make you ill. That is why it is important to address your issues quickly, getting to your Self Counseling within 24 – 48 hours. If you "check out" every time the going gets rough, affirming everything is okay when you know it isn't, you abandon yourself. Instead of masterfully working on the issues you are faced with, you are off in some inauthentic pretend reality that keeps you powerless to make positive changes.

When you ignore your feelings, you are abandoning a sub-personality that is calling for attention and healing. These Inner Aspects are like lost children who need you to acknowledge them. They are crying out for your help and they do this through the emotions. When you don't listen, their voices become louder. If you continue to ignore them, they will find a voice through a physical illness or other challenging condition. You are the only one who can lead your sub-personalities out of the darkness to the light. Therefore, your conscious awareness is essential to the equation.

Christiane Northrup, M.D. believes the subconscious is a significant key to restoring health. In her book, *Women's Bodies, Women's Wisdom* she points out, "Because our emotions often got stuck at the childhood level, a dichotomy formed in our nature. A person can have a PhD and an emotional intelligence of a two year old."

Until you face your issues and deal constructively with your emotions, they will not go away, and you will not know the inner peace that is available to you. You may be empowered in one area of your life, while wounded inner children rule another. You may have a positive attitude, but your life is coming undone around you. I know this, because I used to ignore my feelings, a practice that led to a debilitating illness that almost took my life.

At the time, it seemed like the highest path, the more loving way and yet, in retrospect I see that it was the only way available. No one was teaching a way of going into your emotions. The emphasis was on escaping them. So, having followed what I felt were some of the highest spiritual principles on the planet, I became a master at Spiritual Bypass. Cruising in my higher self much of the time, I felt a great sense of fulfillment and peace but I had no mastery over my emotional self. I did not know how to adequately deal with it, nor did I realize my subconscious was busy creating distress in my life whether I paid attention to it or not.

To deal with the level of heartbreak, upset, and betrayal I felt in two key relationships, I threw myself completely into my work, focusing on the positive while largely ignoring the devastation I was feeling. After some years of this, I became ill. I had two heart attacks within six months and was told I had an incurable heart virus. Not ready to die and leave four small children, I entered a healing journey that taught me a powerful lesson about emotions. When left unaddressed they can quickly become an illness.

If I had understood this powerful part of me could create such a challenging condition, I would have listened to its voice of pain. By addressing the part of me that was in pain, it would have helped me avoid my illness by inspiring me to leave an abusive relationship. By listening to my heart, I would have been more able to protect it, but as so often happens, sometimes we need to learn things the hard way.

The vast body of knowledge I gained from these mistakes led me to my healing journey, and has been a tremendous help in my work with abused men, women, and children. I learned, first hand, the ramifications of bypassing emotions and this knowledge has helped to change and possibly even save lives.

This body of knowledge is especially important for the spiritual community of the world, as it is essential that people today, more than ever, learn how to turn within and embrace their wounded selves without judgment, fear, or shame. When we are courageous enough to go right into the heart of our upsets, we can experience the profound healing and empowerment that occurs from addressing our issues on the deepest levels.

Depending on your level of mastery, this inner work can usually be accomplished in less than an hour. Tracing your emotional upset to the patterns below your conscious awareness, you are able to heal the darkest histories of your past and free yourself from suffering.

As each Inner Aspect is healed, a transfiguration occurs. Your life has transformed from within. You come to a place of understanding and peace, where you experience your full authentic selfhood. Through this radiant Indwelling Presence, you are filled with light, emerging illumined and joyous. You feel whole and complete. You have "enlightened" an Inner Aspect that has lived in pain, misinterpreted an experience in your past, and taken on a pattern that played havoc in your life. You have set yourself free to explore your innate divinity.

Illumined, you enter a creative mode, where you bring your higher awareness to areas in your life calling for attention. You take clear action steps. Where you've lacked boundaries, now you enforce them effortlessly. In this higher state of consciousness, your creative expression flows into wonderful projects. You pour your loving into important relationships, and you dwell for a time in peace, knowing that whatever you may face or go through in the future, you will be able to handle it, because you have TheQuest tools to see you through.

Every pattern you find playing out in your world can be healed, your insecurities, fears, and wounds transformed. You no longer need to live a fragmented life or have dysfunctional relationships.

D.J. Martinovich, a Physical Therapist from Palm Springs, California wrote of her experience with TheQuest saying, "The diminishment of the human condition is based on lack of self worth and esteem, and no amount of verbal affirmation will transform us. It has to come from an Alchemy within. In TheQuest sessions, the very molecules are rearranged, as cells not nourished are now nourished from within. We are truly cleansed from this inner work. This is like a soul clean up, or 50,000 mile check up for the inner being. The best part is that the changes are permanent." A Christian evangelist, DJ had for years spiritually bypassed her own inner pain to stay in loving service to others. This resulted in her body debilitating to such a degree that she had lost her zest for life.

After a few sessions, she was so changed that she now says her life is divided into two parts, "Before Aurora" and "After Aurora." Her health has returned and she has a new passion for life. Even her marriage was transformed. She wrote, "I can't believe how changed I am. People notice a calm and clarity. I have not reverted to the patterns since our last sessions. I cannot think of a better birthday gift than a chance to heal the inner soul of the grief and debris from our years before."

This level of healing and self-mastery allows you to continually transform the challenging aspects of your life, changing it for the better. This is the power of TheQuest to change your life conditions from within. This inner work sets you free to live from your higher nature, in harmony, loving and peace, as an enlightened inhabitant of this world, who in working towards a better future, brings that enlightened vision to the planet.

Healing our patterns is a sacred offering to a world in transition. If we courageously tend to our own inner kingdom of unhealed aspects, others will be inspired to do the same. When more people on earth heal the schisms in their psyches and change the patterning that has run down their family lives, they will live in harmony and peace.

This is how we can heal the earth from within and set the stage for a more evolved future. We can manifest Heaven on Earth, by creating Heaven in our individual life experience. This is the level of mastery our world is calling for, if we are going to turn the tide on planetary challenges and birth a new more enlightened future. This is how we will have a New Earth.

CHAPTER THREE

Finding Your Soul Purpose

Many people on this planet are awakening to their Soul Purpose. Through immense challenges they are catalyzed to profound inner healings and emerge with wisdom, insights, and tools to assist others. Perhaps you've experienced this as well. It is a story I hear all the time. People emerge from TheQuest sessions clear about their Soul Purpose and how they want to fulfill it. As they cleanse themselves of human patterns and are restored to their Authentic Self, they emerge with a gift to share that is powerful.

I saw this with one client who had a long history of abuse. She entered my office with an aura of distress, exhaustion etched upon her face. A highly successful businesswoman, she was being abused by her boyfriend, ex-husband, and her son and was finally at the breaking point. Every area of her life had been impacted by these dysfunctional relationships and she was worn out. "I'm a wreck! I scream at my children. I'm a bad mother. I'm starting to believe all the horrible things my boyfriend, ex, and son keep telling me." Her life was literally falling apart.

TheQuest counseling sessions we did together were powerful and her courage incredible. Each session led us to a horrendous past where abuse, sexual and physical from her father had been a way of life, beginning when she was a young child. We found wounded sub-personalities with low self-esteem that were literally driving her "down to the docks each night" to get a 'little love" from the drunken sailor who had become her lover. A metaphor for her descent from self-respect, this image that one sub-personality provided, helped her see the degree she had been abandoning herself. Craving love, she would come out of each encounter with her boyfriend feeling battered and broken until the verbal abuse had taken its toll. She had lost sight of herself as a beautiful, powerful woman until she finally believed she was worthless and didn't deserve love.

Like most abused people, she tried to break away, but each sub-personality tied her to this man. On a deep subconscious level, she believed her healing could only come through healing the abuser and finally receiving the love she desired. So her sub-personalities reenacted the energetic from her painful childhood, so that they could re-experience this old wound and find healing. But the healing was not in changing him, a long time alcoholic that was not interested in change or in curbing his hatred of women. The healing had to come from within.

Once she had accessed the secret code behind her history of abuse, she was able to set herself free. As each trauma was healed and the subconscious patterning transformed, her life began to miraculously change without any outer effort on her part. Finally, she stepped free from her life sentence of abusive relationships. She emerged from her quest powerful and clear, with a heart for women and children in distress. She felt a deep sense of purposefulness and moved into a career of helping others.

After a year and a half, her life had finally come together in a beautiful tapestry and was now reflecting a harmony and peace that she was radiating to others. She became engaged to a wonderful man without abusive tendencies, showing the pattern had been broken. Her son went through rehabilitation and emerged free of the problems of his past. She moved far away from her ex-husband and dealt with any of his further antics masterfully from a place of inner peace and personal power. She joined a spiritual organization that educates and assists others. Her life had become one of greater purpose.

From this empowered place she shared her sense of victory and the wisdom she had gained saying, "I can see now I chose to experience a childhood of trauma and pain so that I could have compassion for the plight of women and children. I had to get into the trenches otherwise I would never have understood the dilemmas others face, and perhaps I wouldn't even have cared. I had to see things from the inside out. If I had never gone through my own painful experience, I would never have been compelled to help others in the way I am now."

So many of my clients have come to this same conclusion. Afflicted with a challenge to overcome, they end up developing a special gift for humanity. This was definitely true with my illness. While it took years to trace the cause behind my illness and cure it, the journey educated me more than a thousand studies could have done. It gave me the profound awareness of the inter-relationship between our mental, emotional, and physical bodies, and the importance of a holistic approach in addressing every condition. Consequently, this approach brings tremendous results in my healing practice.

One of the most exciting aspects to my illness is that it took me on an exciting adventure into the heart of a region that had barely begun to be explored. The knowledge I gained helped me forge a way to control my emotions, master my psychology, and re-pattern the programming that had limited my self-expression. It gave me answers to age-old questions and an understanding of the psyche that has been of great assistance to others.

As my life was transformed, I saw my family and clients make great strides and experience profound inner shifts. I saw how the impact of my inner work had a powerful affect on the world around me and came to understand that each of us has more effect on the outer world than we realize.

Dr. H. Ronald Hulnick, President of the University of Santa Monica (USM) wrote, "Every time one person resolves one issue, the whole of humanity moves forward."

I believe that all experiences work to our greater good, no matter how challenging. My passion for knowledge and truth were the deciding factors in my fate, for with such a huge challenge to overcome, a quest was born that forged my life purpose. My illness had catalyzed an exploration into the uncharted realms of the psyche where I was able to do pioneering work and emerge with a worthy offering for humanity.

Through the powerful inner work of TheQuest, the mystery behind our present earth dilemma is unveiled. Knowing that there is a purpose behind the many painful experiences we find ourselves in as children born to this troubled world, has given my clients a great sense of relief. When you finally understand the greater purpose behind your suffering and that your challenging life experience was a way your soul devised to cultivate and bring forth your sacred offering to the world, it can free you from the sense of being wounded or broken. It is then you can emerge empowered and free to do your greatest work.

CHAPTER FOUR

Removing The Stains From Your Soul

A woman came to me whose son had died in an unfortunate accident when he was 18. It was ten years later and still this woman could not smile. She carried the loss of her son in her heart and no amount of support groups or therapy had helped her to change her fate. Subsequently, as often happens with long-held emotions, a physical illness developed in her lungs.

The Topping International Institute did extensive studies on the inter-relationship of emotions and disease, which was one of the foundational trainings I received early on. They found a direct correlation between emotions and organs and how an emotion that runs over a period of time can develop into a full-blown health condition in the corresponding part of the body. This is why it is important to resolve our issues quickly so that we don't leave ourselves open to disease.

For me, my unaddressed heartbreak over a couple years translated into a serious heart condition and two heart attacks. In this woman's case, her grief, long associated with the lungs, had caused her physical condition. When we worked with the part of her that had the lung condition, the Inner Aspect revealed the history of her grief, the great sadness she was still holding, and the deeper causes from a previous history that had created the pattern in the first place. For the first time in ten years, this woman felt happy and carefree. Her lung condition cleared up and she felt she had a new lease on life. She was in peace and had finally let go of her sadness around the loss of her son and the painful memories she had held onto around his death, all this with just one counseling session.

Michele Gold, author of *Angels of the Sea* had a similar experience from just one session. She wrote, "I had been feeling very sad, almost hopeless for quite awhile, which is very unlike my Nature, and within 24 hours of TheQuest Counseling session with Aurora, it just lifted... nothing outwardly changed... and yet, I felt happy inside, a peace with where I was at. It was huge. Aurora's healing gifts are very powerful! The energy that had been suppressed inside me came forward and new projects began moving and many new creative ideas were bursting forth. I felt freer than I had felt in many years, happier, and filled with a quiet confidence that was battered for so long, and now was emerging from an ancient cocoon, with new shimmering wings with which to soar."

It's an incredible joy to see great burdens lifted, broken hearts repaired, and people ridden with anxiety moving quickly into peace. The many miracles with this work have given me hope for our world and the knowledge that we can actually make the shift in consciousness required to graduate our present challenging experience and move into a time of peace.

Star Trek has been a favorite show of mine for years and what I love so much about it is that the crew is living in a time when peace has been restored on earth and enlightened actions are the normal way of life. That humanity throughout time has held the ideals of a Utopian World shows that this vision is encoded within us. It is part of our innate design, and it can become a physical reality if enough of us do the inner work to make it so.

There are a lot of challenges to face and many hurdles to overcome, but we can do it. We can become conscious co-creators of our reality and birth a Golden Age on Earth. The first step is to tend to our inner world of unhealed aspects and human patterns. When we remove the shadow imprint upon our soul, we can emerge as enlightened individuals who can positively change the world around us. This innate destiny is within us to fulfill. We just need to clear the way so that it can manifest its glory in and through us.

We came into this world pure and innocent. Once here, we became tarnished by life's painful experiences, losing sight of who we are. We believe we are victims in a sad movie. We feel we are ruined and can't be repaired. Author, James O'Brien, PhD spoke to this phenomenon in his book, *Silver People*. He described how Silver People once were Golden People, but life challenges and painful childhoods changed them to silver. He wrote, "My earliest childhood memory is kissing the cool, smooth forehead of my mother, who had died a few minutes earlier. That's the kind of memories silver people have. Our hearts tarnish and turn cold when exposed to the tragedies of life. We envy gold people. Your hearts ignite when you enter the fires of pleasure or pain. So even your bad memories keep you warm."

At the time he was writing Silver People, Dr. O'Brien had a series of counseling sessions with me that allowed him to heal many facets of his "silver personality." In one of these landmark sessions, he uncovered the core wound that had turned him from a golden child into a Silver Person. His powerful healing is a testimony that Silver People can be healed and transformed, that we don't need to live in pain or continue the patterns of our past. I share his full story in Part 5. Miracles of TheQuest.

At last there is light at the end of the tunnel. Even though we may feel wounded, tarnished, broken, ruined or destroyed, we can be restored. We can remove the stains from our souls and emerge unscathed from the worst circumstances to fulfill a high destiny no matter what we've ever been through.

CHAPTER FIVE

How To Shepherd Your Shadow

The most challenging aspect of human existence is the Shadow Self. It is the part of you that lives below your conscious awareness and yet it is behind all the challenges you face in life. It is responsible for your ill health, disempowering relationships, financial constraints, and a host of other conditions, all of which affect your confidence and self-esteem. To be living your highest potential, you need to learn how to shepherd your shadow, while empowering your Authentic Self, so that your higher nature can be the leader in your life adventure and the author of your destiny.

The Authentic Self is a lost treasure within that must be excavated and, the Shadow Self is standing in the way. It must be healed and transformed for you to realize your greater potential.

Brad Onsgard, a Police Officer and High School Teacher in Aspen wrote, "Dr. Ariel's method of going inside one's self and healing past issues and gaining self-realizations is really quite amazingly simple, yet very valuable. Almost like finding a key to a hidden treasure."

In each age we have seen the shadow being the most dominant part of human consciousness through wars, pillaging, murder, and rape. Humanity has not reached its full maturity, nor has it come close to realizing its full potential. That potential is yet unexcavated beneath layers of human conditioning. A victim to the fate of human patterning, humanity has been compelled to seek a way out, but much of this quest has been in the outer sense, tending to each little problem, while the deeper causes remain unaddressed.

People are so overwhelmed by the human condition that they long for God to make everything right. Even the most enlightened teachers have barely made a dent in world affairs because of this programming.

The planet has become a world of turmoil to such a degree that the Garden of Eden has been relegated to a faint flicker in human memory.

Many people today are too overwhelmed by their own limitations to believe that they can make any real changes in the planetary equation, so they look to others to do it. Meanwhile, their Shadow Self keeps adding to the world dilemma. Subconscious patterns have such a hold on their perceptual reality that they finally believe their capacity is so much less than it really is. They've not only gone under the amnesia inherent on this planet, they've become over-identified with their personality traits, addictions, and problems, never realizing that there is a greater part of them, a magnificent part that is yet unrevealed and untapped.

While religions are filled with ideals of a transformed world, nations of people wait upon a savior to set the world right, because they feel powerless to make these changes themselves. But even our most illustrious saints have fallen under the weight of the Shadow Self.

Sages throughout time have sought truth and many of them became illumined, but the Shadow Self, while tamed, has never been completely vanquished. Jesus, in a fit of rage, turned over the table of the money changers at the Temple and other enlightened or wise personages down through history have similarly displayed their Shadow. Enlightenment has been such a fleeting experience that many could not stay in peace for long. There was a part of the human psyche so huge, so strong, and so compelling that it would overcome them when least expected. Humanity has forever fought against this shadow, felt shamed by its presence and overcome by its dictates, but has been powerless to overcome it... until now.

In the last century, we watched countless gurus, ministers and spiritual leaders attain huge followings and fame, only to have their ministries come undone by this shadow aspect. "Falling from grace," their personality failings have played havoc in their otherwise spiritually advanced lives. This mystery has confounded many devotees, who after following religious leaders in a host of rituals for spiritual purification, believing they will soon be "enlightened" or that they are "saved," witness a play of human patterns in their teacher that causes them to leave the group shattered and disillusioned. Many have wondered, "Is there no way out of the human condition?"

Standing Bear of the Manataka American Indian Council believes there is nothing more important than becoming free in mind, body and soul from modern confusion in order to reach a higher plane of spirituality. "Our very survival depends on it. To see the Light of the Rainbow we must quiet our minds and feel the inner peace and strength that flows as a river, one with nature and all creation." But how do we accomplish this? How can we quiet our minds and feel the "inner peace and strength that flows as a river" when we have bottled up anger and uncontrollable rage? How can we walk the Path of Light, when we are troubled with the personality afflictions of our Shadow Self?

The only way out of this dilemma is through directly addressing the wounded part of us, because left ignored, the shadow will work havoc in our lives. We have myths and metaphors around this part of us. We have called it the devil and projected its presence outside of ourselves. We have had so much fear around it that we want to drive a stake into its heart and bury it beneath the earth so it can no longer affect us, but repressing it only causes it to get stronger and more virulent.

Like a tidal wave, pent up emotions crash into our lives, destroying the wonderful things we have created. They explode like volcanoes, covering our shattered lives with an ash that tarnishes our hearts and turns us cold. If not healed and resolved, our emotional responses to life become turbulent waters we can barely navigate.

One spiritual group calls this shadow aspect the Dweller on the Threshold. They believe it is an evil part of us that is continually out to destroy us. These people live in fear of its presence, not knowing that the Shadow is easily quelled and that it is providing a forum for us to attain greater self-mastery. Therefore, it is an active agent working towards our greater good even though it wears the appearance of evil.

Compassionately approaching the darkest parts of ourselves is the only way we can lay to rest the history of pain that has plagued our human existence. We've been afraid to face our darkness, believing it is who we really are. That is why TheQuest tools are so effective. They shed light upon the pathway, making the journey easy and safe. When we finally emerge, the healing of a shadow aspect is complete.

When people believe in an inner or outer evil that is out to get them, they can never relax and be at peace. Even if they are distracted for a moment, there will always be an undercurrent of fear running in them. Such has been the great travesty of the belief in a Devil that tortures humans and whose wrath God subjects sinners to by relegating them to hell.

We've seen beliefs of this nature in witch-hunts where people believed the Devil was among them. Whipped into a high state of frenzy, groups of religious citizens were driven to heartlessly murder innocent women. Looking back upon this genocide, it is clear to see the "devil" was in the initiators of this great travesty, not the women who were burned at the stake. The Shadow Nature had taken over and was the principle actor in the play.

There has been so much fear and shame around our shadow nature and yet, after generations of accumulated patterns traversing our family lines, the truth is, we all have a Shadow Self. No one escapes this! Similar shadow patterns run through every family line, adversely affecting each family lineage. The good news is that the Shadow Self allows us to experience many facets of life we never could have on an enlightened planet. Personal challenges and relationship dynamics teach us in ways that nothing else can. As spiritual beings having a physical experience, we learn and grow and evolve from our earthly dramas.

The Shadow Self exists in our psyche and there is no escape. It is part of the planetary dilemma, and the source of all the ills humanity must continually face. Each innocent child who is born into this world inherits it. To walk in this world as enlightened beings, we must learn how to shepherd our shadow. The longer we allow each drama to play out, the more we reinforce our subconscious patterns and perpetuate the pain from our inner wounds.

The key is to work on your issues as they arise. It is then you can heal a core wound that has kept you in dysfunctional relationships and attract a healthy relationship instead. You can shorten the time of suffering by quickly healing the patterns responsible for your pain. You can become a master of your psychology rather than a victim to your shadow. In the words of one client, "My life is very changed. I am showing up different in my relationship with my husband, my son and others. TheQuest has brought me a renewed sense of faith in the Divine."

Meditation and yoga can soothe the soul and help you get to that place of peace within. I've found both to be essential elements in maintaining a healthy lifestyle. They continually bring me back to the place where I can experience and express my true nature. They reinforce and sustain the powerful experience of who I truly am behind all the programming and upsets, and give me a reference point of peace when the going gets rough. Having this empowered vantage point makes it easier to see when the Shadow has been activated, and helps you to skillfully tend to its healing.

The reason why humanity has yet to gain its full maturity is because its missing potentiality, the 90% scientists speak of, is yet untapped and therefore not accessed. It has become lost, held disempowered in the Shadow Self. Locked down in the chambers of the psyche, your sub-personalities hold all that you lack, all that you long for, and all that you wish to become. Like a treasure trove waiting to be uncovered, the truth of who you are must be reclaimed from within for you to be fully empowered in the world.

To access this treasure, you must focus on the facet of your life that is lacking. Perhaps it's love you seek or greater wealth. Maybe it's a cure to your illness or the healing of your relationship. You may be working on these things believing the outer effort is all that is needed, but there is a faster more efficient way. The reason there is lack in your life is because of a shadow pattern, so the way to have what you want is to change the programming. Otherwise, you may attain these things only to have them washed away like castles in the sand. When you add the inner work to your action steps and outer efforts, you greatly increase your ratio of success. The shadow aspect that is longing for love believes it is unworthy of love and so is keeping love away. When you heal it and other aspects that are in charge, you create an opening for love. By healing the patterns that are creating the challenging dynamic in your relationship, the love and harmony is restored. By transforming the programming that has relegated you to a lesser income, you clear the way for greater wealth.

Until now, there has not been a key to unlock the door to the psyche or even the knowledge that if that door were unlocked, we'd find a treasure chest within that would give us everything we could ever desire. We have stories of genies in bottles, but we haven't realized that the genie is our Authentic Self and a part of its power is lost in a Shadow Self that needs to be restored. We have floundered through our life experiences unaware that the Shadow Self must incrementally be restored to its innate design for us to manifest our full potential. There are tarnished facets of our beings that need to be excavated and then polished until they shine. We must access the lost power in this disinherited part of us to bring an end to suffering on earth.

When we trace the history of Golden Ages past, we see how far the world has descended from its former glory. There are legends of an awakened humanity that once lived on the continent of Lemuria, a Garden of Eden spectacular beyond belief. Then, a serpentine nature entered the psyche of humanity, forming a Shadow Self that caused humanity to lose its Edenic consciousness. Whatever the history of our lost heritage, humanity has forever been seeking to regain the lost paradise of its authentic selfhood.

A mass exodus from shadow belief systems is taking place, as people around the world seek to find their lost selves. A quest, familiar to the saints, sages, and medicine people throughout history is underway by millions of modern day mystics who are seeking to know their true purpose in life. This Great Awakening brings humanity the opportunity to vanquish the Shadow Self from our world, through an "Alchemy of the Ages," that could end suffering on earth.

CHAPTER SIX

Healing Your Core Wound

Healing our Shadow Self is not the work of one day. It is the journey of a lifetime. It is a destiny calling us to restore our lives from within. The more we understand our Shadow Nature, the more at peace we can become with our human patterns.

Each one of us carries a core wounding. It is the dilemma of being born on earth, a part of the planetary equation. No one escapes this. Each of our family lineages carry within them a subconscious patterning of pain that cycles out into world affairs, creating many of the dire conditions we experience on earth. The influence of this wound is far-reaching. Its ramifications can be seen in lack, poverty, illness, and war.

Each of us must look within to find the core wound within the psyche of our family. This wound will reveal itself in troubling family dynamics, personality dysfunctions and limiting life circumstances. No matter how healthy you or your life may seem, if you have a family member who is abusive, addicted to substances, has financial troubles, or is the "problem child," this is a clear indicator of a core family wound that must be addressed by each person in your family.

Like the alcoholic who cries his endless victim stories while unconsciously abusing others, the "troubled" one's life will mirror the depth of inner pain within the psyche of the family, while displaying the "unconsciousness" that is part of the family pattern. This inner voice of pain will continue to pour out its sorrowful tone through troubled family members, their illnesses and dysfunctional lifestyles, until each person in the family learns to go within and address their own inner pain. While you may have chaffed at the circumstances around your family dynamics, the voice of pain has one purpose, to call you on a journey of self-discovery into the heart of your core wound so that you can heal it for the last time.

The painful voice of a family member holds the key to this core wound. By listening, rather than ignoring the pain of this person, you can begin to hear the voice of your own inner pain. You may not play out the same wounded role as a troubled family member. You may not be addicted to substances, an abuser, get angry easily, or go on a tirade when things go wrong, but if you look deep enough, you will find where your own inner wounding has had its effect. Perhaps it has caused a low level depression or feeling of being shut down that has dampened your enthusiasm, creativity, or ability to feel joyous or loving. You may have formed barriers around your heart and pushed love away. You may lack self-esteem, feel insecure, or lack confidence. This may have caused you to become a workaholic.

We have not only looked at family members as if their pain is foreign, we've also failed to comprehend that everything we see mirrored in the outer world, including the patterns and behaviors of others, can be found within us. Hard working achievers will never look like the more ineffectual family members because their accomplishments will continually be applauded. That is because our society loves Super Achievers. The more people wear themselves out accomplishing great feats, the more they are heralded in the world as pinnacles of success.

I was once a workaholic. Saddled with responsibilities and feeling overwhelmed by a host of projects, I finally had to reflect on why my life was looking this way? In my excitement to achieve my goals, I had lost one essential ingredient, the ability to relax and enjoy the blessings of this earthly existence.

I found that beneath my Super Achiever Pattern was an inner emptiness that traversed my family lineage. Though my drive was based on noble humanitarian ideals, at the root of this drive was a deep wounding. Through a series of Self Counseling sessions, I healed this inner wound and extricated myself from its workaholic patterning. I was transformed from an A type personality to what I call an AB type, proving personality traits can be changed. I can still get things done in a timely way and work hard over long periods of time to accomplish a goal, but for the most part, I am living a balanced and healthy life, with time for friends and family as well as fulfilling projects.

If you are a workaholic, if you are constantly driven and cannot relax, if you never take time out for yourself, it is important to take a look at what is really going on. To do this, you must look within to see what drives you, what is behind your need to accomplish and achieve. While achievements in themselves are thrilling adventures and, believe me, I love them, when your life goes out of balance to achieve something and this goes on for a long period of time, you need to look at the deeper cause. You may be carrying the same inner coding as a family alcoholic, bearing the same core wound while compensating for the disease in a different way.

A workaholic lifestyle is a similar pattern to that of an alcoholic. Work and constant activity become the addiction, and both are ways people check themselves out from what is really going on inside. Unless addressed, these patterns will continue to traverse the family line, infecting each succeeding generation. The perpetuation of the family wound will continue to be inherited by our children and children's children. Translated on a global scale, suffering will continue as a normal way of life on earth.

Through TheQuest Self Counseling, you can unlock the puzzles of your life and find answers to your dilemmas. As you trace each pattern into the past, you begin to understand your psychological make-up; how you took on the family patterning and carried it forward in your own life. You will see how this pattern is being played out in your relationships and daily affairs, and how it is being mirrored in an imbalanced lifestyle that reaps disappointments and personal failures.

If your past is riddled with alcoholism or drug abuse, if you've been the troubled one in the family, the so-called Black Sheep, you may have a great sense of shame and not realize that the pain you are carrying inside of you was inherited from the family pattern. Driven by your addiction to unconscious behaviors, you may have hurt others but if you never go within to find out why, if you never address the pain that is inside of you, you'll never be completely free of your addiction. Your addiction is an attempt to bypass your emotions and stay out of touch with the deeper cause. It's too painful to feel, so you reach for the bottle, you pop the pills, and soon it all goes away. But, it never really does go away. There's always that aching pain inside just beneath the surface. There's always a world of troubles just beyond that closed door. There's unhappiness behind that smile. No matter how much you indulge your senses, the core wound never goes away.

The parts of you that have the addiction need your assistance. They live in a wilderland of pain and are seeking comfort from the storm. They turn to food, or become shop-a-holics. They keep you running like rats on a wheel. Whatever their modus operandi, they deserve your compassion. They are like wounded children trying desperately to cover over their pain.

Overindulgence in food that creates weight conditions is one way Inner Aspects try to protect themselves. They may have drawn in an abusive relationship, or were abused in the past. The person may be losing something dear to them or undergoing a challenging experience. Adding all those layers onto the body provides a false sense of security.

To lose the weight, you must heal the part of you that hurts, and release the accumulation of pain you've been carrying. In her recent interview with Oprah, Valerie Bertinelli confided how some people measure their depression by the medication they take or the number of times per week they see a therapist. For her, she measured her depression with baked jalapeño-and-cheddar-cheese poppers. Valerie gives us a glimpse of her addiction in her book, *Losing It*. She writes about the nights she "OD'd on the poppers, burning her mouth because she couldn't wait for them to cool down." She confides that those were some of the "darkest days of her life and she was eating her way through them." She lost her smile and her weight soared past 170 lbs. After *Touched By An Angel* went off the air, she became a hermit, "hiding from the world hoping that no one would notice she had become fat." She finally realized that she was hiding from the one person who could help solve her problems, herself!

Like many women, Valerie tried every diet she could find, but once she stopped the diet, the weight would return. This is because the deeper cause had not been addressed. Finally, she did the hard work. She confronted the fears, insecurities, disappointments, and frustrations that accounted for her fluctuating weight. After that, it was just a matter of self-discipline and exercise. Adding diet and exercise to her inner work, the weight came off. She surpassed her goal and had a renewed zest for life. Kirstie Alley had told her she would quit hiding and discover the real person behind the weight, and she did. She got her life back. Like Valerie, when you get to the heart of your addictions and heal the patterns in charge, you reclaim your life.

Carl Rogers, the Founder of Humanistic Psychology and the pioneer of Client Centered Counseling believed that living the good life was not for the fainthearted. It involves stretching and growing, becoming more of our full potential. It involves the courage to be all of who we are and to fully launch ourselves into the stream of life.

David Gershon and Gail Straub, in their book, *Empowerment, The Art Of Creating Your Life As You Want It* say that to create a healthy emotional life, you have to let go of the deep hurts you are holding onto from the past. To have peace of mind, you have to release your anger, resentment, and bitterness.

Understanding your patterns and how they played out allows you to face your own responsibility in a world filled with suffering, and in family dynamics where you once thought the troubled person in the family was the only wounded one. Finally facing the core wound within, you can heal it for the last time and release yourself from dynamics that have caused suffering down your family line.

Unlocking the mystery of your family lineage is empowering. It is incredibly freeing to move past the inner core pain to see the meaning and value it brought to your life. It is then you can finally understand its many gifts. You will have a new level of compassion for yourself and others because you suffered or were oppressed. The ability to empathize with the plights of others could even lead to fulfilling your Soul Purpose. Sharing your new awareness can be exciting when you've made a journey that can be a light to the world.

Shakti Gawain, the author of *Creative Visualization, Living In The Light* believes we are living in both an exciting and challenging time. Humanity is facing overwhelming problems and yet, more than ever before in history, we have the opportunity to transform our lives and our planet. We can meet our present challenges powerfully and effectively through shifting our consciousness. Whatever we do individually has a profound impact on us all.

If we want to heal our lives, the core wound in our family lineage and our world, we must take this journey within no matter how scary it may seem and no matter what it may uncover. As Confucius said, "To put the world in order, we must first put our own nation in order; to put the nation in order, we must put our own family in order; to put the family in order, we must cultivate our own personal life; and to cultivate our personal life, we must first set our hearts right."

CHAPTER SEVEN

The Final Step: Healing Your Addictions For The Last Time

It is still relatively unknown that we can heal our addictions. This is one of my most important discoveries and why I have so many results with this therapeutic approach. We don't need to be a workaholic our whole life, we can actually become an A/B type person that can get a lot done and enjoy life as well. We can heal the patterns behind our overeating and drop our excess weight quickly. We can learn how to live a more balanced life. We can stop our addictions and have peace of mind and better health. It's really very exciting and simple.

I've seen such a dramatic response from this work because TheQuest goes right to the heart of addictions and heals them at the root cause. Not only is it an excellent way for people to change their life, but TheQuest also provides a missing piece that can dramatically increase the success rate at rehab centers, addiction, youth at risk, prison reform, and other programs. It can be available at health centers, retreats, and spas. It can be incorporated into high schools and colleges. The ramifications of this work are great. It can change lives worldwide.

In 1995, I was in Aspen setting up a model chapter that could be duplicated around the world under the Institute of Advanced Healing, a non-profit organization I founded to bring out TheQuest worldwide. The chapter included a weekly Teen Forum for Youth at Risk, a Healing Circle for adults, and classes at local high schools for teens. Ninety nine percent of my clients were addicts. Cocaine, gambling, pornography, marijuana, alcohol, cigarettes, you name it. The level of addictions that ran rampant in that valley amazed me. This is one of the most pristine, spectacular places on the planet. Everyday people are out running, biking, hiking, and skiing. They are so health minded and athletically inclined, I could not believe how many people in the area were suffering from addictions.

The level of pain my clients were holding in their psyches revealed what was really at the heart of their addiction. Beneath the physical needs and psychological cravings were sub-personalities that were part of a core wounding driving people to cover over their pain. These sub-personalities had the addiction, not the client. Working with many addicts over this time period, I found that when I isolated the sub-personalities contributing to the addiction and systematically healed each one, the addiction would just fall away on its own. Even the person's cravings would disappear, because the addiction was a means to an end, not the core problem. When the underlying causes behind an addiction are addressed, a complete healing can take place.

One client had used marijuana for years, but when he stopped he became angry and abusive. Tracing the cause behind his anger, we found a wounded inner child (and corresponding parts) whose rage had grown to such a degree that he was unconsciously using the drug to keep these feelings down. For years he had smoked marijuana from the time he woke up in the morning to when he went to bed at night, completely oblivious to the fact that there was a problem. He thought he just loved marijuana, but the real truth was he was using it to check out. Being a "nice" person, he had adopted a way to keep his anger locked inside.

Over many years, the underlying pattern had created ever-new experiences that added to this rage until it was huge. When he decided to clean up his life and stopped smoking marijuana, the pain, long pent up inside of him, came to the surface and burst out of him in a tidal wave of rage. In just three counseling sessions, we were able to get to the heart of his addiction, heal the wound the marijuana use was covering over, and stop the anger.

There has been a tremendous amount of research and work bringing us to this point in time, where at last we are finding a cure for psychologically based afflictions. Many programs have done a fabulous job in helping people trace the history of their addictions and see how they are affecting their life. It's a powerful way to educate yourself and I wholly recommend and, you can go further. There is a missing piece to the equation that can tremendously increase your success in breaking free.

It is the final step, where you heal your addiction for the last time.

Deep within your psyche lie vats of teeming emotions. Like cauldrons bubbling over, they hold the records and memories of your painful past. These are parts of you that are deeply wounded, parts that feel great anxiety or pain, parts that live in fear or doubt, and these are the ones that have the addictions, not you.

Many institutions and rehab centers still believe addiction is incurable and consequently they are only having an eight percent success rate with addicts. This is because the subconscious is not being addressed. While many aspects of these programs are helpful, without this missing piece, the individual can easily fall back into the addiction once the stress level increases. Major life challenges have caused many addicts to fall off the wagon, because the pattern behind their addiction was never healed. Until an addiction is completely cured, there will always be the tendency to fall back into addictive behaviors.

The people who overcome their addictions in these programs have been able to "will" themselves off substances, while the majority of people remain trapped in the lifelong affliction. Labeled as 'a disease that can't be healed,' the focus has been on education and behavioral change, while the subconscious has been left out of the equation. To date, it is relatively unknown that we can heal our addictions and so, many people throughout the planet continue to suffer. Lives are destroyed, relationships are ruined and loved ones, children, and families barely survive the devastation.

There are many types of addictions, not just substance abuse. Being a workaholic is an addictive way of life. Checking out in front of the TV is another, though most people never realize they are addicted to television. You may be addicted to sugar, video games, overeating, shopping, gambling, or pornography. Anger problems and violent tendencies are addictive behaviors. Negative thinking, hypochondria, and even "suffering" to get attention can be an addiction. Some people are addicted to drama. Others become addicted to a person and stay locked in an unhealthy relationship. No matter how badly they are treated, they can't seem to break away. The other person has become a drug they can't live without.

If you have lived with an addiction that has become unbearable, if you've tried to break away but it has you in its grip, if you feel you can't go on, there is a way out. You don't need to live in pain or be saddled with a life sentence without parole. Now there is a master solution to your dilemma and a key to set you free.

TheQuest Seven Steps go to the heart of your addiction and heal it at its root cause, setting off a shift in consciousness that changes the very molecules of your life experience. No matter how entrenched you are, no matter how devastated you feel, or how miserable you've become, in each session you can experience relief. Increment by increment, a deep and profound healing will be taking place, bringing you to that moment in time when you are completely free.

Whatever the addiction or behavior, face it squarely. Honesty is essential. If you ignore or deny anything is wrong, you will never get help and your life will never change. You need to go right to the heart of your addiction and to embrace the part of you with the affliction. In that moment, you will have turned the key to unlock the door of the prison. With such a powerful and easy method to apply, you no longer need to live with addictions, anxiety attacks, or depression. Even suicidal tendencies are easy to change. These are all related to the same inner pattern and are a wake-up call, pointing you to a wound deep inside that is ready to be healed.

This is your opportunity to wring out all the emotions that have held you hostage, twisted your life, and caused you so much pain. Each sub-personality is a voice crying out in the darkness from within your psyche. Each addiction can be a catalyst of positive change. Right now today you can take the first step to heal an addiction or behavior that has been a destructive element in your life. You can embark on a quest for healing and know you are taking positive steps to create a better future. There is a light at the end of the tunnel. Follow it! There is a new horizon beckoning to you. You can reach it! It's right there waiting for you, but you must take the first step.

To effectively deal with your addiction, you must be a wise manager watching over your life. You must move into action the moment a craving begins, and find the sub-personality that is driving you. Then, apply TheQuest formula, taking the Inner Aspect through the Seven Steps. Remember, it is the Inner Aspect having the craving or driving the addiction, not you. So you can take command and help it.

Strengthen your will. Extricate yourself from people and situations that reinforce your addictive behavior. Join a support group.

Ask your friends for help, and do your Self Counseling each time you feel you need to use a substance or fulfill an addiction. This will take effort. Addictions are not healed in one day, unless of course you are destined for a miracle, and those do take place. They are not easy to heal, but it can be done, and it will take you on a very interesting and deeply fulfilling journey.

From that glorious mountain valley in Colorado, I felt an amazing elation knowing how huge this breakthrough is. It is a miracle that addictions can be healed, that we can free ourselves of circumstances that once seemed beyond our control and conditions that seemed incurable, that we can release ourselves from the pain we've carried for so long. TheQuest can alter the very nature of the future of humankind on this planet.

I stand here with great expectation and a prayer in my heart that this body of work finds its way into the hands of every person on earth it is meant for, so that every wound in every one of us can be healed. This is my prayer, my blessing, and my offering to the earth.

Part Five

Miracles of TheQuest

CHAPTER ONE

Birth of TheQuest

For years, my focus was on mastering spiritual practices in the hope of attaining the highest adeptship, but while I reached incredible heights in consciousness, my emotions played havoc in my world. I could not control them. And no matter how much I wrestled with patterns and personality traits, I could not free myself from them. Neither could I end the recycling of painful relationships, financial constraints, and personal hardships.

While I was living all the highest spiritual formulas for success in positive thinking, daily affirmations, meditation, and healthy diet, my life kept coming unraveled. What I built I lost. What I attained spiritually disappeared in moments of frustration or anger. Though I held the highest ideal for my relationships, they would consistently be so much less than my visions and dreams. Heartbreak seemed to be the reward of an exemplary spiritual life, rather than happiness and success. I could not understand this. Wasn't I doing everything right?

Seeking to stay in my "higher consciousness" through a severely painful relationship, I had become a master at spiritual bypass. When, without warning, I had two heart attacks within six months and was told I had an incurable heart condition that could quickly debilitate me to death, my life was changed forever. I had received my wake up call. My spiritual practices and higher state of consciousness were not enough.

Mortally challenged, I began to look deep within myself to find answers. This led me into the psyche where I discovered heartbreak was the cause of my illness. Through that journey, I gained an understanding of the inter-relationship between emotions and disease. Going deeper still, I found the patterns behind the challenging conditions I had faced and why I had drawn in a relationship that had been so heartbreaking. This helped me understand the challenges I had encountered in life and how my subconscious patterns had created everything of a dire nature

I had ever gone through.

I also learned the value of listening to my feelings and supporting myself when going through something difficult, attention that I would have naturally offered to one of my children, a client, or a friend, but somehow had left myself out of the equation.

My greatest discovery was finding the Authentic Self at the core of my being, not something bad, dark or evil. In each session, I would discover this Self beyond every pattern and human emotion. Instantly, I would be filled with love, understanding, and compassion. I could finally see myself in my true state, a powerful spiritual being having a limited human experience.

I began to have a more conscious relationship with this part of me, who many times appeared in my inner sight as a radiant woman emanating light. I learned that her intention was to fulfill my every dream, vision and desire, but to receive her gifts, I had to clear the way in my subconscious. I also had to release control. As I did this, I became more 'enlightened' and free.

I became an adept at resolving my issues quickly and healing their underlying patterns. I was a Master Alchemist moving from upset to peace quickly, shortening the time of misery I would have gone through by dramatic degrees. I was freeing myself fast from every painful condition that appeared in my life. Increment-by-increment, the human patterning was dissolving as I cleared the way for my Authentic Self to manifest her vision in my life.

By healing my patterns, I found I was also clearing my family lineage with its history of pain. Finally, I understood why the planet looks the way it does, why so often we fail to bring our enlightened self into the equation. The world keeps reflecting the inner wound of humanity, while the Authentic Self remains lost beneath this programming.

Everyone on earth is run by subconscious patterns to a lesser or greater degree. To get off this endless track and manifest a higher vision, we need to address the inner causes to our life dilemmas. When we release ourselves from suffering, our victory ripples through the collective helping others break free. We are all connected in the Circle of Life. Our healing helps to heal the psyche of humanity, and changes the world around us.

So many times, I've risen like a phoenix from the ashes of devastation and despair. Through the hardest experiences, I learned how to restore myself quickly, and return to my Authentic Self. These challenges also translated into years of delving deeply into the psyche, where I made many landmark discoveries. Through this pioneering work, I developed my Counseling Theory and Practice, TheQuest. The mastery I gained on my personal trek became TheQuest Life Mastery Path I teach today under the Institute of Advanced Healing.

My son, Aradeus also become adept at TheQuest. In my book, *Earth 2012: The Ultimate Quest*, I share how I trained him over a year and a half, where we gave each other back to back sessions each week. He was the one who inspired me to distill TheQuest into a seven-step process that could be taught to others. This totally resonated with my vision of handing this knowledge to the layperson, instead of just to practitioners, as is normally done.

Aradeus and I began holding a weekly Teen Forum and gave classes at local high schools in Aspen and the valley, taking the kids and their teachers through the Seven Steps. I was amazed to find they loved it! I was also holding a weekly Healing Circle and watching people's lives change. This was very heartening. It showed me that anyone can use TheQuest to do their own self healing process. A complete Self Healing System had been born.

By training Aradeus, I began developing TheQuest Master Counselor and Spiritual Leadership Training. Today it is a one-year certification course. It is an exciting journey with my students, where I pass my knowledge to them in a way that is experiential. As they encounter life difficulties, I Life Coach them, passing on essential information to help them understand what is really going on at deeper levels. Then we do TheQuest Counseling to clear the way.

Step by step, session upon session, they extricate themselves from painful conditions. They gain Self Mastery by applying TheQuest in self-counseling sessions as their issues arise, an important part of the program. Upon graduation, they are not only masters of their psychology, but they have an exemplary skill as a Counselor and Life Coach that can help others. They then have the opportunity to transfer this knowledge to their community by setting up a chapter of the Institute there.

TheQuest Healing System provides a missing piece to rehab and addiction programs, prison reform, youth at risk programs, and to many afflictions humanity is facing today. Excited by the ramifications of transferring this Healing System to others, I designed TheQuest

Counselor Training so that anyone can take it no matter how busy they are or where they are living in the world.

TheQuest University's mission is to pass this Healing System to individuals who are destined to take it to their communities around the world. I see counselors from different programs mastering this technology and rapidly changing their clients' lives. I see it being taught as a college course and in high schools.

TheQuest brings the missing link at a time when humanity must awaken and take its place as a wise steward of the earth. It is a key to finding our Lost Identity, for it awakens us to the Authentic Self that lives at the core of our being. We then remember our true heritage, our Lineage of Light beyond the human programming.

Through my own arduous journey, I proved a way of Self Mastery that is empowering and life changing. No matter what circumstances we were born with, or how ingrained our patterns or addictions are, we can take back the scepter of power and change our life.

This is the Path of the Initiate. By mastering our psychology, we become Adepts in the New Millennium. Our inner focus and healing work has a rippling affect, touching lives throughout the world. By transforming our life, the world is transformed around us. By living more often in our Authentic Self, we anchor Heaven on Earth in our own life experience, and pave the way for Eden to manifest its glory on Earth.

CHAPTER TWO

Out Of the Darkness Into The Light

I had spent years on a roller coaster watching in anguish as my eldest son's life and sanity unraveled from substance abuse. This broke my heart and caused so much stress that there were times I could barely handle it. Sometimes the weight was unbearable. Of course, guiding him to a substance free life was an impossible quest. I finally realized that he was the only one who could heal his life, and that would only happen when he was ready. No one can compel us to do anything!

Things finally accelerated to where I thought I would lose him. The use of drugs and alcohol had taken their toll and he had become delusional, depressed, and suicidal. After three days straight on drugs without sleeping or eating, violence erupted in a fight with his girlfriend and she got hurt. Much was revealed as she poured out her painful story, my daughter and I listening silently by the speakerphone, tears flowing from our eyes. I was devastated to learn the dark places my son had entered over the past year caused by prescription and other drugs he had been using. I finally had to face that he was not well and this was so hard, because he is so talented and exceptional in every way.

She was brokenhearted that things had escalated between them into harsh words and violence. She loved him very much. She spoke of how she had been living in dread that at any moment he would die of an overdose, and how morning after morning she would come to his window and look in, scared that she would find him dead.

As she shared, my daughter and I had the same premonition at the same time. We saw my son standing over his girlfriend in remorse. He had pushed her down and accidentally taken her life, and then he took his own life. We sat there in shock. He had already gone three days without sleeping and eating, overdosing the pain medicine his doctor had him on. He was not in his right mind. Violence had already taken place. It could easily happen again.

When we realized we had both seen the same vision, we immediately moved into action to 'save their lives.' This culminated in reporting the 'fight' to the police and his subsequent arrest, which he will probably never forgive us for. With the arrest, came a ray of hope dependent on the courts remanding him to rehab and into psychiatric care he had avoided to that time. We were relieved.

Now there was a chance he would get help, but then something unexpected happened. A backlash of anger, outrage, and blame was thrown at us from his grandmother, uncle, and father. Even though he lived with his grandmother and uncle (on his father's side), they seemed to be in complete denial about his rapidly deteriorating condition, how violent and angry he was becoming from the drugs and that he was an addict. Lives were in danger, but they couldn't see it.

Enter A Dark Night

In the days that followed, I felt sure I was going to lose him. Everything had taken its toll. His girlfriend had shared how he had been increasingly morose and suicidal from the prescription drugs, and his already damaged liver had been enlarging in pain with each substance abuse. I knew he was on his way out, but there was no way for me to reach him. He had cut me off.

TheQuest helped me release the trauma and fear. This brought me back into my proactive self quickly. In an inspired moment, I wrote an appeal to the court, asking that they help him by remanding him to rehab, telling them I felt his death was imminent and that the arrest was my son's last ray of hope. I also shared what an incredible person he is. As I wrote, my heart felt like it was being ripped open and seared with intense pain, and this anguish and my love for my son poured into the letter. I wouldn't know till much later, what a powerful effect it had.

In the midst of this devastating experience, my daughter was rushed to the hospital with a tonsil abscess that alarmed the doctors so much they put her on 'watch.' If the infection moved to her lungs she would immediately die. And then I learned my mother's cancer had returned. As if that were not enough, the stock market was crashing and a major investor in my company took a hit, stopping funds that were essential for my company. Without them, I didn't know how I would be able to get my work out to the world. I was just months into the launch with my first book and solo music CD newly released, and was working on book two and a new music CD. Now it looked like I was being stopped in my tracks.

In that moment, the glorious future I had been envisioning where I was reaching people across the earth with this body of knowledge became uncertain, and I had to wonder if I would be able to fulfill the Destiny I was born to and which I have worked towards all my life.

As the stock market was plummeting, people around me were falling under the weight, frightened or in despair. I could feel everything they were going through to such an immense degree, it was almost unbearable. With the added stress of the planet's financial world coming undone, my only resort was to retreat into silence and do my Self Counseling with TheQuest.

Over a couple weeks, I had three profound sessions, emerging with such clarity and peace that I was amazed how positive and proactive I felt each day in the midst of such personal and planetary crises. It was an incredible feat to be this peaceful, artfully making my way through so many devastating experiences all at once.

This Dark Night gave me the ability to see the level of mastery I had gained through TheQuest. Each session brought me to the realization that the immense challenges in my life had been the most powerful catalysts, especially my experiences with my son.

I'd spent years striving to assist my son in his plight, knowing TheQuest could make a great difference in his life, but though he had access to these tools, he had rarely availed himself of them. Instead, he had been in the grip of ever challenging circumstances, overcome at times with anxiety, depression, and other mental problems caused by years of substance abuse, dwelling continually in victimhood, and continuing to make life choices that took him further and further into darkness, while I stood by in despair. At these gravest times, TheQuest had been my saving grace. The revelations in my sessions helped me realize that he is in the driver's seat and I really have no control over his life choices. This helped me to let go increment by increment and became an essential key to reclaiming my own inner peace.

A Way Out

The horrendous experiences I've had to endure over so many years with my son, literally drove me to find a way out of the misery, heartbreak, and pain. Through each self-counseling with TheQuest, I was able to restore myself quickly from the immense stress the worry, fear, and concern caused.

During one excruciatingly painful period in 1999, my son had entered a drug-induced psychosis for months ending up in suicide watch in jail after being arrested for attacking someone. This experience drove me to the brink of a nervous breakdown, but once again TheQuest saved me. Here I was going through the worst of what people have to endure and was restoring myself so fast, people around me were amazed. They'd see the anguish, grief, and despair. They knew I was on the edge and then, I'd emerge from my session clear, calm, and directed, making wise decisions that would help the situation or at least, help me to endure it.

An Extraordinary Meeting

In the midst of the latest Dark Night, an extraordinary thing took place that dramatically changed my perspective about my son's plight. After yet another session, I sat under the stars and spoke to my son's soul before I went to sleep. I released his life into Divine Hands, knowing that I must let go, because there was nothing more I could do. He had been released from jail with his trial pending and saw me as an adversary and someone who had tried to ruin his life.

His future was uncertain, hanging in the balance. I knew I could hear at any moment that he had lost his life through suicide, a drug or alcohol overdose, or through liver failure. There was only one ray of hope and that was if he was sent to rehab and I had come to realize, it was in Divine Hands, not mine.

In the middle of the night, I was awakened to an unexpected experience. My son's soul was standing before me, shining with a peaceful radiance. He took my hand and began speaking to me. He said, "No matter what happens, I am OK. I am always in peace. You need to understand that my earth experience is like putting on clothing that I wear for awhile, but these clothes are not who I am. Eventually I will tire of them and return to my Real Self. They give me an experience that I can learn from. The darkness I've entered has helped me traverse a realm that I am exploring that is not part of my True Nature. It is what I've come here to experience, even though you have seen a greater potential for me. This allows me to grow and expand my knowledge and understanding of aspects of the dark side of earthly life. But nothing I go through, nothing I encounter, no matter how dark the depths I traverse or the degree of darkness that overcomes me will be forever. When I leave this earth, I will be restored. I will enter a place of healing and I will study and review my life and all that I went through. I will go over every experience and gain insights and understanding that no other trek could have afforded me."

I wondered, "Does this mean my son is going to die?"

He smiled at me. I realized then, that his True Self had been speaking to me. I saw how often I had been sad, because I had believed he was losing, ruining, or destroying this Self. I was in awe. The Creative Genius that had inspired me so often and which I loved so much was still intact. No harm or ruin had come to him!

A Love That Never Dies

My son's loving nature and exceptional intelligence had made him special and unique. Even though the past 16 years had been interspersed with drug abuse, accidents, arrests, alcoholism, drug induced psychosis, and subsequent mental problems, there had been so many times when we cruised together like eagles, loving being together and sharing deeply about the mysteries of life. We had delved deeply into healing arts and played in multimedia projects. We shared a love that is profound, that transcends time, and spans lifetimes.

This was the person I knew and loved, not the tortured, angry and abusive one who would spew his wrath at me. This was the alliance I believed in and knew was rare to find on this earth. This was the soul connection that had graced my life despite the times he had turned on me and accused me of horrendous crimes that never took place from his drug induced delusions.

Though this anger and abuse only took place once a year in the beginning, these episodes had increased in the past two years to such a degree, I knew I was losing him. But, despite all this, his True Self would emerge at times from the darkness. Then he would meet me in this amazing Love we've always shared, the true reality that has always existed between us. At those times he would speak of the power of our connection and that I was the most important person to him in his life, his greatest mentor, teacher, and ally, and the person he's learned the most from. The love and understanding between us would be profound. Each time I would have renewed faith that he would be OK, but then the dark cycle would begin all over again.

To watch his True Nature replaced by a person who was angry, demented, suicidal, and abusing drugs had been too much to bear. Now, from this amazing encounter, I was seeing how many times I had bought into these earthly dramas, alarmed that he would be completely taken over, convinced that if it continued he would die young, and knowing that I would not be able to handle it. It would ruin my life and I would never recover.

He smiled at me and said, "You know how strong our Love is. This love will always be. It is our special bond. No matter what happens, you need to remember, I am eternal. This is but one life in a span of lifetimes, each with their unique experience and learning opportunities. I will always return to who I am. That will never be lost because it is the core of my being and everything else is just experiences I cloth myself with to learn."

I found myself relaxing, but still fully aware this could mean he would die soon. My mind did not want to go there. It was too horrific to imagine. I would not be able to handle it. I would be devastated, feel great despair and regret. I would always feel there was something more I should have done or that I had not done enough. I would have let him down. Because I had seen what great potential he had, I would always feel his death and demise was not right. He had been meant for so much more, a great destiny to fulfill. His death would be too great a loss.

He continued, "You will never lose me. Our love is too strong. We will always be close. This is one moment in an eternity of time." Tears poured from my eyes as his love penetrated my being and for a time I basked in the truth I had always known, that we share a unique bond, a special love that has never been ruined no matter what we've gone through and no matter how many illusions about me have flooded his mind or how horrendously he has treated me, it was never destroyed.

Healing

I became aware of a pervading sadness that had permeated my life and how strongly it had infected me below my conscious awareness. I had caught glimpses of this Sad Soul at times, as had others. In fleeting moments I would look in the mirror and catch sight of her. Beyond my lighthearted personality was this deep secret. I was a sorrowful soul who had barely been able to make it through all I had endured.

I saw her standing before me. She carried a weight that was too much to bear. Her body was bent over and she was in dark colored rags, impoverished by all the strain and strife these experiences had etched upon her life. She had not been able to feel a true happiness all the years my son was undergoing his trials. Instead, she had been in constant fear, alarm, worry, and concern for him. Each sad event had left her troubled and broken hearted. She had also been affected by the suffering of others close to her and by the immense suffering on earth.

This dark element in my psyche had kept me from being truly happy or having an authentic smile from deep in my soul. How could I be happy when my son was suffering and in danger, and when so many people close to me and across the world were in pain? How could I live in a transcendent peaceful reality when they were struggling under such dire circumstances? It was a cross I had been born to carry and with it, a strain that was hard to bear. This part of me could barely handle the suffering in the world on top of all the suffering of my loved ones. It was too much and I had barely made it through. How could I find happiness on a planet when all this was going on? It had finally taken its toll.

He drew closer. "Trust in our love and know that everything I've gone through has been my choice. It is important for me. Remember who I really am and will always be. It is the same with everyone. Each person has this Authentic Self they will return to in time. Therefore, you do not need to take on the burden of what they are passing through. You can live in your Authentic Reality as you have been doing, and shine that light upon the world, for this has been a great strength to me. Through everything I've passed through, your strength, your ability to be your Authentic Self most of the time has helped me immensely. I could go deeper and deeper into the darkness knowing I was connected to you and that you were holding in the Light. This gave me the ability to venture deep into the dark side of my nature knowing I would never get completely lost, because you were always there showing me the Authentic Self that is my innate truth."

He continued, "Because you were in my life, I could never lose myself, even though I lost touch with my True Self so many times. You know this is true, because no matter what I've gone through and no matter how dark I've become or deranged, I have had lucid times where we have communed as we are doing now. I am the part that you've held to, believed in, known was there, no matter how scary things became. You never stopped believing in me for you knew the truth. You know who I really am, and you have never lost sight of me. Because of your strength, because you've held for me through everything, I had an anchor to the light. Because you could see the Real Me, you helped me know it was there."

A shift in perception began taking place within me as his perspective illuminated my mind. I turned to the inner woman, knowing it was time for her to be healed. I could not continue to bring my work out to the world and be the shining light he had acknowledged when she was inside me feeling this way. At last I had found her and now it was time to release her from her pain.

I saw how she had stayed fixated on my son's demise and this had broken her heart. She looked like the pictures of the saints with a sword piercing her heart. Now she was seeing the Truth. She saw that his Eternal Self was unharmed and knew he would come through unscathed, no matter what he went through, no matter how great the darkness, no matter how much it looked like he had lost his soul.

A huge relief rippled through me as she began to lighten. Finally she was ready to transform. She had gained so much from her horrendous life experiences. She had sought the cause of suffering and found a cure. She had proved this in her own life and in many others, and now she was bringing TheQuest technology to the world. If she had not undergone so much, she wouldn't have had such a fire to accomplish all she had or possibly even cared that there was so much suffering in the world.

I emerged from the experience secure in the knowledge that my son and I share a Love that will never die, because it is our truth. Even if he dies young, I can see that we will eventually meet again in the higher realms, once we are back 'home,' and that all will be right between us. We will be restored from the ravages of this earthly life and our bond will continue secure. Nothing that can happen in this world can change that. This has brought me great peace.

Letting Go

I've now let go to an amazing degree, knowing that my son is in Divine Hands. There is a divine part of him that lives forever in a reality beyond this earthly experience, that is always there for him and that he can forever rely on for the Truth.

I cannot deny him his earthly experience, even though I've wanted so much more for him. Who am I to say what his life should look like? After all, it is as he said, only one out of many lifetimes. Through millennia of time, we grow and learn from our experiences. Each one is unique and important, each essential on our soul evolutionary path for a particular learning. They may seem wrong, but are they really? Maybe everything is always working towards our greater good and we can never lose who we truly are.

The next month I experienced what I suspect others go through when a loved one passes on. You long with all your heart to be with them, to experience the love, the bond, and affection that now is lost to you. I realized, "I'm grieving!" I had lost him as I know him. He had shut me out and continued on his path in denial about everything. I felt what everyone must feel, when they lose a loved one. You hope that it won't be too long until you meet up with them in Heaven… but now I have an inner peace knowing that will happen someday.

I emerged from this experience with a new sense of lightness in my heart. Happiness returned I thought I had lost. I was finally free from the stress filled roller coaster ride I had lived for too many years. My attention was redirected on bringing out my life's work and taking care of myself rather than everyone else. The biggest miracle of all was that, against all odds, I was able to complete the book I had been working on (# 2 in the Earth 2012 series), release it and go on tour, and then complete this book in time to gift it to the world on my birthday, August 25.

In the midst of all this, I had the most amazing awareness. I realized that what my son had done was really an Act of Love rather than a heartless thing. By pushing me away, he was protecting me from more years of pain having to watch his demise. In that moment, I felt his Presence with me. He was looking at me with so much Love. I felt it enter my heart. It was strong. Nothing we had been through had ever ruined it and nothing can. In Eternity, our bond has never faltered. This is a love that never dies.

A couple months later, I received a call from the Prosecuting Attorney about my son's case. My letter had greatly impacted the public defender, who saw how much I love my son and how desperate I was that he get help. He inspired my son to plea bargain, and showed the PA my letter. This inspired her to help, by giving him a year of outpatient rehab, NA meetings, an anger management course, and probation where they would drug test to help keep him on track. For the first time in many years, there was a ray of light shining on his pathway!

I could hardly believe my letter had such an impact, the PA was calling me herself. I could tell she was very pleased with the outcome and the role she had played. I expressed my gratitude that she had given him a chance to heal his life, and told her what a beautiful and amazing person he is. She concluded with, "God bless you."

A blessed light rained over me and I felt there was hope for the first time in years. Maybe now he could overcome the substance abuse. In the following days, an inner awareness showed me the future had been altered. A power triad had formed when my daughter, his girlfriend, and I had aligned in support of his soul. In that moment, everything had changed. His dark path had ended. A new future path had formed and he was now walking on it. Despite the greatest odds and adversity, my son's life was extended. What he does with it, will be up to him. My daughter and I are in peace, knowing we reached out at a moment of great danger, and pulled him back from the jaws of death.

CHAPTER THREE

Redemption

I had cruised in absolute bliss for some time, immersing myself in writing, and feeling empowered and freer than I had ever been from my last healing with the situation with my son, when a new episode began that would call me into another deep and profound change.

It began with a series of emails from a female student from Israel who I will call M, who had recently visited her home country after a year in TheQuest Master Counselor and Spiritual Leadership program. She had made great changes as she did the work and had written a glowing testimonial of how TheQuest had changed her life. Session upon session, she was becoming free of old programming that had caused a lot of distress and unhappiness, especially in her relationship.

As she reentered the US, she was interrogated by Immigration for six hours while her boyfriend worried on the other side, not knowing what was happening. She didn't have the right paperwork, something I had in the past said she must have, but she hadn't listened. Now she and her boyfriend were blaming me, as I had been the one working on her Visa under the Institute of Advanced Healing so she could be in the US to receive this training.

We found out they had denied her, but for some reason, they had botched up the Institute's new address and we had never received the letter. Instead of taking responsibility for her own actions and waiting to find out the true reason for the denial, she and her boyfriend launched a host of false accusations and character assassinations. This caused a hit financially for the Institute and myself at a time when I was relying on this income to support me while launching my life's work.

As the drama accelerated, I went deep in my inner process. Session upon session, I used TheQuest to heal my sense of hurt and betrayal, and kept emerging clear and directed, which helped me to write loving emails to help resolve the situation, but they stayed locked in their position. I had just been editing the story by Joe Vitale on

Ho'oponopono in my second book, Earth 2012: Time of the Awakening Soul. Ho'oponopono is a Hawaiian ritual of forgiveness that Kahuna, Grandmaster Pang, had trained me in. This is a very powerful ritual of release that helps clear negative energies, cuts the aka cords that keep people in negative dynamics, and helps make things right. The Kahunas teach that everything we encounter in life is a reflection of what is going on inside of us. Therefore, our challenges are our responsibility, no matter who out there seems to be doing it to us. This had become the premise of my life's work.

Redemption Through Suffering

That night, I began seeing how all the people who had been hurtful in my life had been a reflection of a part of me that was being mean to myself. I was working with an Inner Aspect that was ready to step into a New Life of greater abundance, happiness, and fulfillment. She was standing in the darkness looking out through a doorway to this new pathway and she was in great pain. She had lived forever this way, being loving and kind while others crucified her. She was punishing herself in this way to 'redeem' herself for her past transgressions. I traced these and found the self-judgments she had carried from all the times she had unconsciously hurt others or made mistakes. This had added up to a huge loss of self-esteem, and had literally transformed a blessed life into a nightmare so many times in my past. Now I had found the part of me that was carrying this pattern, who was enforcing a path of suffering, and who was implementing it with all the strategic success of a military general.

I began traversing the past, seeing each person who had harmed me. People who had stolen from me, lied to me, taken from me without being able to give, men who had abused me, fathers and others who had abandoned me, friends who had turned on me, assassinating my character and turning others against me. As I faced each person and reviewed the painful past I said, "I forgive you. I am sorry. And, I forgive myself." This is Ho'oponopono. A way of taking responsibility for what we draw into our life, and then releasing, letting go, thereby 'cleaning' our past.

I kept feeling freer and freer as the hours passed. Finally I lay down in my bed ready to go to sleep, seeking to find anyone I had missed, and there was more. I woke up the next morning and the

Ho'oponopono continued. Interspersed with this forgiveness work I was having huge realizations. I was really getting how each harmful person was a reflection of a part of me, and how I had drawn these situations in to punish myself. I returned to TheQuest to work with the Inner Aspect in charge. She was reviewing her life history and seeing how much she had abused herself. She had created grave challenges where she had been heartbroken and cast out. Friends had turned their backs on her and people had treated her unkindly, while she had been loving and a true friend to them.

She was seeing how her idea of redemption through suffering had caused her so much heartbreak and pain, and how she had become that idealized martyr that some religions think is the highest offering we can give to God to redeem ourselves. She was awakening to the truth. Living a harsh existence had taken her away from the qualities she knew were God, like peace, love, harmony, happiness, and abundance.

There was also an upside. Through many hardships in my life, I had learned to be good to myself, to be my True Friend, and session upon session, I had used TheQuest to heal my past and release myself from patterns that created suffering, never realizing I had forged a way to redeem myself. This was Ho'oponopono, True Forgiveness of Self.

I marveled at how this present horrific experience was serving me, as other challenges had. How the worst people in my life have given me the greatest growth and learning, and if it had not been for them, I would never have found this Path of Redemption, nor been able to free myself of this legacy of pain. Now I was uncovering a crucial piece in my life history, a deep core wounding I never knew was there. This had played out through so many scenarios and people that it is an absolute miracle my pure heart and loving nature stayed intact.

TheQuest had over the years restored me from these hits, cleared the deep sorrow and pain they created, and removed the stains from my soul. As I had done this work, I kept feeling younger and lighter, until I never looked my age again. I had learned to dwell in the part of me that is always joyous, alive, and passionate about life, who loves deeply and is a true friend to others and to myself. I had forged a way of freedom that I was sharing with many. My experiences had all served a grand purpose.

Redemption Through Healing

Now I was with the woman in black standing at the open doorway. The New Life looked awesome, a radiant vision of abundance, opulence, and peace. Quite a stark difference from the times of financial constraint and misery she had known.

I longed to step through the doorway and leave this momentum of pain behind, but she was not ready. She wanted to talk to me and so I listened. She said, "I have lived like this forever, for I am in all humanity. I am in women who have suffered greatly in this world, been denied their rightful place and freedom to be all they are. I have been at the heart of indigenous cultures whose ancient heritage was wiped from the Earth until they rose up with all their might to reclaim and restore it. I have been the innocent child who is abused by the father she loves, breaking her trust in men and creating a lifetime of painful relationships. I have been the child who was beaten and who became a violent abuser to reclaim their power. I have been the sorrowful soul who has covered over their pain with substance abuse, the millions who suffered genocide, who have been trampled under and misused. I am the one who suffers and must keep suffering to redeem myself. So my legacy has been written into all the world religions as the path I must take to be redeemed. But now, I am tired of suffering. I am tired of this history of pain. I am tired of being small, manipulated, and used. I am tired of being cast out and made wrong when that is not the truth. I am tired of having every good thing I create destroyed. I am tired of illness, poverty, and strife. I can no longer live this way."

I looked on with great compassion, seeing the many histories and people she spoke of in a living movie that wrenched my heart and tightened my stomach. I felt it all as if it had been me, every last history. She smiled with a radiant purity and took my hand. "I needed to show you," she said. "I needed you to know the truth. This is a world of suffering and now you know why. It is not that God has willed it so, or that we are prisoners in a hell created for sinners. We have been lost in a wilderness of beliefs that make it so, that create the very reality we would escape from, and we never knew why. Humanity doesn't understand why, but you must tell them. You've come through all of this so that you could show them the way out."

Tears of joy streamed from her eyes as she took my hand. "Now we can ascend this sad movie, for it is time. You've learned enough through this arduous trek. Now it is time to live the Abundant Life that is the Divine Intention for you and every soul on earth. From that new vantage point, you will illuminate the way for others."

She was transforming before my eyes from the sorrowful woman in black to a radiantly beautiful, shining woman who was now stepping through the doorway into her New Life. I sighed with relief, knowing how huge this was. It was one of the most powerful, landmark moments in my life.

I reflected on the cruel behavior of my student and how she had served me to claim this victory today. I saw how everything of a dire nature in this life had turned me to the Light and how each horrendous experience had driven me back to my Self, that bastion of light and love within me. Could the worst people in my life really have been my Saviors, helping redeem me from a painful past? Each had highlighted a dark history that had been set in motion by false beliefs so that I could set myself free. All the good people in my life had just left me as I was, whereas the mean people had catalyzed my deep inner work, and that had resulted in victory upon victory. I saw then that they had been the ones who had helped move me into fulfilling my Destiny of bringing TheQuest to the world. I was amazed.

A huge wave of relief passed over me and I shuddered from deep within, as the change took place inside of me. I was being redeemed in the only way that is True Redemption, restoring the Shadow Aspects back to their Divine Nature. In that bastion of peace, I can honestly say, I'd come home.

My Inner Aspect was now standing in the citadel of True Authentic Power, wielding a Scepter of Truth that represented all the knowledge she had gained. A golden pathway opened up before her. It felt warm beneath her bare feet. She was in a luminescent long white flowing dress and her heart radiated love out to the world. She smiled from deep in her soul and radiated pure love from her being. She had released herself and was free. I watched this happy scene, as opulent pictures formed around her. This was the Abundant Life, a place of safety and peace where true fulfillment could be found. This was a way in which she could drink in the best of life and also walk a pure and saintly path. This was the true meaning of redemption. As the soul is restored, it becomes pure like snow, and I had found the way.

CHAPTER FOUR

TheQuest Session That Saved Three Lives

By Kaitlyn Keyt

I had been consciously and physically raising my Vibrations for over a year. One morning as I was getting dressed, I literally heard a voice say, "Today is the day you are ready to heal some major obstacles that are needed to clear, so you may move forward on your purposeful path." I went out into the day expecting just that to happen.

Sure enough, as I walked up to the New Age Retailer booth at the International New Age Trade Show in Denver, Kathy, the editor of their trade magazine introduced me to Aurora saying, "I don't know why but I am suppose to introduce you two. I feel very strong about this. There is an important reason you two are supposed to know each other."

Immediately Aurora and I began to share about our work. When I heard about TheQuest I had a strong feeling I needed to experience it while Aurora was excited about my VibesUp Energy Raising Tools. So, off we went to do a trade.

About 2 months prior to meeting Aurora I was at an event where I had someone read my aura and then take a look at my palm. He said, "Oh! There's a fatal car accident!" looking at the lines on my hand, and than gulped and tried to change the subject.

I said, "I haven't been in an accident."

"It hasn't happened yet?" he replied. He looked chagrined.

In the days that followed, I kept trying to get that experience out of my head, but now I know I needed to get it out of something much deeper than just my conscious thoughts.

My session with Aurora was not only life changing, within hours it literally saved 3 lives! I prepared myself for the session by placing a couple of my VibesUP cylinders on the front and back of my heart area. I know that stuck energy moves faster when it is in a higher vibration, and this was the basis of my work, to create products that would quickly raise people's energy.

Aurora was incredibly skillful as she walked me through her process. We went to the root of some core wounds and patterns that kept me attracting more of the same hurtful experiences. Then something amazing happened. As the wounded feminine part of me was being healed, the wounded male aspect that had been in the dynamic with her came into my awareness, ready to be healed as well.

I had for some time been aware of the importance of healing the wounded feminine we all carry, that suppressed intuitive side of us that has been dormant for far too long. Yet I was not aware of the 'wounded' masculine, which is the logical side of our brain. I was amazed as both came forward to be healed and than merged together as a team bringing their powerfully positive sides actively into my awareness. I felt this amazing connection between the two within a renewed whole self.

That night I was driving with my precious family. As the light turned green, I headed into the intersection, but 1/3 of the way through stopped for no reason. A feeling had come over me to stop, which normally would have been overridden by an analytical response from my 'male side,' a pattern I had for years. It was amazing that 'all of me' was OK with following this inner feeling and holding still in the beginning part of the intersection in the middle of traffic!

Without warning and before I could think about what I was doing and why, a speeding car zoomed through their red light and missed my car by a few feet. Had I not stopped, we would have been t-boned at a very high speed. I sighed in relief, realizing immediately that my beautiful 12 yr. old son would have taken the brunt and most likely been killed by the impact because of the speed of the other car. I knew in that moment that I had literally changed my life course in my session earlier that day with Aurora, a lesson in my path I no longer needed to experience, because I had gone to the root and healed it. My rational mind was no longer in total control. Room had been made for my intuitive feminine self just in time.

I remembered then, that I had also been forewarned a year earlier that a fatal accident was showing up in my astrology. It was something I had to be very careful of, and yet I would have met this fate had I not been guided to meet Aurora and have TheQuest session, which altered my future before it could take place. When I look at my son, I am so relieved and feel so much gratitude that Kathy listened to her inner guidance to introduce me to Aurora, and for Aurora's help in shifting my destiny that day.

Aurora's life work is so important! I believe it is not just our conscious thinking that attracts events and circumstances into our lives. Healing the root of the old wounds that continue to send out signals, attracting back more painful lessons and anchoring us to a life of suffering is vitally important at this time. We are currently in an experience of Body Mind and Spirit. They all affect each other. Raising the Vibrations of our physical bodies and environment is my work and I believe this helps us to attract the perfect healers and synchronicity on our path like I did that day with Aurora.

We are constantly being dragged down by our vibration-polluted airwaves, water, and food, so raising our vibrations is important. When our vibration is high, our healings and conscious work can be far more powerful and effective, helping us journey back to our True Glorious Self.

Kaitlyn Keyt, Founder of VibesUP, *speaks internationally on rising above outdated fear based belief systems and joyfully stepping into the Higher Self. In her words, "Our thoughts, emotions, and our beliefs affect our Vibration and what we attract into our lives. Great News! Nature can absolutely help on our Journey of uplifting and healing our lives and our planet."*

Kaitlyn has created a fun and powerful line of over 30 natural Vibrational Therapy products. From Vibe Bracelets that tune you into 18 specific energies to Vibrational Therapy Teddy Bears. Her favorite is the Divine Soles, earth energy shoe inserts, which instantly balance chakras and take you back to your natural state of being, helping you see above the fog of your artificial environment and creating space for a smoother healing journey.

For more information see http://www.VibesUP.com. For discounts and special sales, put in code # 216.

CHAPTER FIVE

Doorway To a Cure

When one of my sons was five, the doctor told me he had a serious growth hormone deficiency that could severely stunt his growth. It became a serious dilemma when the insurance company would not pay for the daily growth hormone shots he needed to reach his normal height. The cost was way beyond my ability as a single mother, at $40,000 a year. It was a very challenging situation and I was determined to find a cure.

As with everything I've faced in life, I take my dilemmas to a deeper level. I also use natural healing methods to cure every illness, and had great success with everything my four children contracted over the years. They rarely needed a doctor except for check ups because of the healthy foods, environment, and way of life I raised them in. My natural healing methods quickly cured serious conditions like bronchitis and high fevers, but this was a huge challenge way beyond my ability. My son's body was not producing enough growth hormone to bring him to a mature height and this was out of my league, or so I thought.

One day I felt inspired to take him through TheQuest and to my amazement, an extraordinary history was revealed. I was focusing on why he was not growing. What was this block to growth? Immediately, we tapped into an Inner Aspect who was holding a core belief, "I don't want to grow old." The Aspect took us back into a journey through distinct experiences, all with a similar theme.

This belief had created a pattern that had literally formed a physical condition that was keeping him from physically 'growing up.' Working with the Inner Aspect that was holding this belief system, we were able to heal the pattern.

Subconscious patterns affect our physical reality. At the core of these patterns are the beliefs we took on from misinterpreting our life experiences. These form the patterns that are behind our life challenges. They etch their imprint upon our physical world and body. At the heart of every illness are patterns that are calling to be addressed and healed for the last time, so the conditions they create will stop reoccurring. This then changes our future. We no longer need to go through the challenging experiences our beliefs and their patterns dictate. We can transform them and step free.

Within three weeks of this session, the doctor called with unexpected news. He said, "I don't know why and I am not going to ask, but out of all of my clients, your son is the only one the insurance company has approved for treatment!" I was stunned!

We had cleared the way and now my son was able to receive the treatment he needed. A miracle had occurred from our reprogramming his subconscious. Consequently, the insurance company paid hundreds of thousands of dollars over the next years and my son grew to his normal height. We even had a second miracle after that. A time came when we no longer had insurance and were in the same situation where I could not afford the medicine. The Company was notified about our situation and provided my son with the Growth Hormone shots for free.

I truly believe that if we had not done this inner work and reprogrammed this belief system in my son, none of this would have taken place, and he would have been relegated to a very different life.

I continue to see miracles from this work that defy reality and yet, when you understand the inner working of the psyche and its power in our outer world, it all makes sense.

CHAPTER SIX

Fat Crippled Orphan Boy With Glasses

Author, James O'brien, PhD spoke of the phenomena of how people become tarnished by life's hardships in his book, *Silver People*. He described how Silver People once were Golden People, but life challenges and painful childhoods changed them to silver. He wrote, "My earliest childhood memory is kissing the cool, smooth forehead of my mother, who had died a few minutes earlier. That's the kind of memories silver people have. Our hearts tarnish and turn cold when exposed to the tragedies of life. We envy gold people. Your hearts ignite when you enter the fires of pleasure or pain. So even your bad memories keep you warm.

At the time he was writing *Silver People*, Dr. O'brien had a series of TheQuest sessions with me that allowed him to heal many facets of his "silver personality." In one of these landmark sessions, he uncovered the core wound that had turned him from a Golden Child into a Silver Person. His powerful healing is a testimony that Silver People can be healed and transformed, that we don't need to live in pain or continue the patterns of our past. There is a way out, a light at the end of the tunnel. Even though we may feel wounded, tarnished, ruined or destroyed, we can be restored and emerge unscathed from the worst circumstances.

Dr. O'brien has now passed on, leaving a beautiful legacy of knowledge behind him. He had experienced such profound changes with TheQuest, he was inspired to share the following story about one of our sessions together. In his words…

My first session… "Wow! Aurora is such a beautiful and magnetic woman! I'll just concentrate and look into her beautiful eyes, and try not to notice the rest of her."

At first, Aurora and I talk about my trust in her and her expertise, and also my fear that I might lose my creative 'edge' if I heal and transform some of my negatively judged parts, whose traumas are important to the book I'm writing called *Silver People*.

I decide to trust that the process will not turn me into 'a boring bland guy from Des Moines,' and go forward, trusting Aurora's guidance. We pray and ask for the help of Mother Mary and all concerned divine beings. I mention including my own Divine Self.

In the session, I identify my 'Fat Crippled Orphan Boy With Glasses,' as the cause of the background sadness and lack of confidence I feel many times. Then I recite a poem about him and how I've judged and not accepted this part of me. Here is the poem.

Fat Crippled Orphan Boy With Glasses

I remember
Waking up each morning
In the boys dormitory
Everyone still sleeping
Except me

Pressing trembling hands together
Fingers flat against fingers
Happiness flooding through me
Thinking, I'm not a fat boy anymore
Only to discover
Sadly to discover
That I still was
What I still was
Fat crippled orphan boy with glasses

Even now I feel him
Wandering deep inside me
Crying deep inside me
Lonely deep inside me
Waiting for me to love him
Still I do not love him
When will I ever love him
Fat crippled orphan boy with glasses

Fat Crippled Orphan Boy With Glasses

As the years continue passing
Many wives and lovers dancing
Just to share their love and passion
Trying to love that orphan boy

But he waits for me to love him
Knowing that I can't forget him
Though he knows I can't forgive him
For the shame he brought upon me
And the love he drove away

Still he waits for me to love him
Knowing I can barely love him
Waiting patiently for me to say
I love you now
Come with me now
Fat crippled orphan boy with glasses

    We discover that my Golden Boy Period ended and my fat period began after my Dad's death when I was 11, and ended at 16, after I was adopted at 15. So "Jimmy", this part of me, was trying to comfort himself with food and get some notice as a bigger guy who had value for that! Since then, Jimmy has been trying to protect me by discouraging me from doing things or going after what I want, so I won't be hurt by failure or rejection by people. He says "hold back, don't ask anyone for anything, don't love or trust all the way with anyone, you can rely only on yourself."

    Prayers of Self Forgiveness help me to release my judgment of Jimmy and to have compassion for what I went through and why I went through this period. I find that Jimmy's purpose in my life was to teach me how to rise above such challenges and still be a happy, loving person; to be able to have compassion for people with challenges; and to be able to have many people relate to this story and learn this lesson as I bring it out in my book, *Silver People* and other things I do.

    Understanding how important and essential this life passage was for me, I thank Jimmy, who now transforms from the fat, crippled orphan boy, whose job was now over, to the Golden Boy again. I do feel that a major shift has occurred inside me. I haven't noticed that sad/not good enough feeling since. I can easily visualize that golden glow now, and it feels great!

CHAPTER SEVEN

More Miracles Of TheQuest

In the following personal accounts, the miraculous healing theme continues. Through TheQuest, lives were healed and circumstances transformed. I share them here, because I feel it is important that we understand that no matter what we are facing, the deeper patterns behind our struggles can be healed, and the challenges we face can be transformed. There is an innate part of us that is ever working for our higher good. The more we allow it to manifest its intention in our lives, the more we can live in Heaven on Earth in our own life experience.

- 1 -

My Relationship Was Doomed For Failure

My experience with TheQuest has been amazing. I had been doing sessions for about 6 months and I was very changed. Life had changed tremendously too. My relationship with my partner, which is my business partner and my life partner, turned from a dysfunctional relationship, fighting daily, lacking communication, not satisfying and very unhappy to a communicative and more enjoyable loving relationship. My stress levels were reduced about 50% and my business became more successful. I felt more ready to have my baby.

The most amazing session I remember, though each one is amazing since each one solves another "mystery" that was keeping me unhappy, was at the beginning when I realized daily fighting with my partner is not normal.

We used to fight every single day and not once, but two to four times a day. After telling my partner about the session and how I realized I fight with him because fighting was what I used to see my parents do most of the time, most of my life, we realized that his parents used to do the same thing, fight with each other every day.

Both of us were keeping our parents' pattern alive in us. In that moment, we decided we were not going to be like them. We were going to solve our problems by communicating and discussing without fighting. Since then we fight maybe once a week if that. That's after 3 years of only fighting, and many times a day.

Aurora has changed my life. TheQuest is something I want to continue to be a part of. I want to help people like Aurora helped me, to show how they can change their lives, resolve their issues in less than an hour, teach them how to do this in their own life, and that's the reason I'm learning to be a Master Counselor. –Michal Cohen, Israel, Student in TheQuest Master Counselor and Spiritual Leadership Training

-2-

From Chaos To Peace

At low points in my life, I turn to book stores. I was in such a place, staring at the shelves when the owner asked how she could help. I stated what I thought I was looking for, and she gently turned me towards her three latest books by known authors.

I was drawn to Dr. Ariel's book, *Earth 2012: The Ultimate Quest, How To Find Peace in a World of Chaos*, because a word in the title matched my life condition, chaos. There was also the word 'peace,' which I so desired. Immediately I opened the book and began to read getting this rock solid feeling, like when you know everything is going to be alright. This was the book I needed.

Upon returning home I quickly read the book. The words spoke to me of gentleness and kindness, no blame, so simple to follow. I was amazed, and reread several chapters at once before putting the book down. As life returned to my normal chaos, I would pick up the book and reread several chapters finding comfort. I slept with this book on my bed for weeks, awakening in the middle of the night to read yet again and find comfort. I found myself returning to this book again and again as my chaotic life returned, finding peace in TheQuest seven steps. There is no right or wrong, no blame, just transforming emotions.

The book remained on my bed to have close at hand in the night. This went on for six months when I realized I wanted to not only change my life but help others find a way to change their lives also. I became a nurse twenty five years ago thinking it was a helping profession, and it can be, but is hard to accomplish in today's world of turmoil. Nursing has become for me "until the next crises" for the patients I see return with even greater problems. I mustered up the confidence to e-mail Dr. Ariel and much to my surprise I received a reply. Today I am a student of "TheQuest." I now feel I am being taught a way to guide the client away from the condition of dis-ease.

Just a couple months ago I was living in my rapidly deteriorating world of chaos, searching for peace. After two sessions with Dr. Ariel, I felt so empowered. My thoughts were clear and focused. Now, decisions are being made by a strong person emerging with her Authentic Self, ME!

While in session, it is the most wonderful feeling to see the burdens you have carried fall away. Emotions shift, bringing joy and a lightness to your being. You find the root cause of your problem and it is healed. Each time I emerge rewarded, with a clear realization of my problems, and insights into how I can make positive changes in my life.

TheQuest has changed my life. Now I can see myself five years from now and I have a plan! I can now change anything in my life that is not serving me and this is helping me reach my goals. Already TheQuest sessions have made me stronger. It is easier to make difficult decisions and walk my own path.

TheQuest gives seven simple steps the client can take with them forever. Whenever they need help, it will be there for them. Thanks Dr. Ariel for giving this technique to all in need of help. *-Linda Camarata, Nurse, Phoenix, Arizona*

- 3 -

A Miraculous Cure

I had a physical deformity from the time I was a little girl. By continually aggravating the condition through a very active and full life, it became a life long affliction. By 25 years old I had to stop running, a great passion in my life! I also loved to ski, hike, and bike, but my knees would get so sore that my lifestyle was greatly hindered.

During TheQuest Life Mastery Training Course in Aspen, I had the opportunity to work with Dr. Ariel. In my session we traced a pattern back to my early childhood where I had suffered severe abuse. This was something I had not remembered and yet, in the session I could see how it had affected my whole life. As we unlocked and healed the pattern, I felt a tremendous release.

The very next day I was working out at the Aspen Club gym when looking in the mirror, I noticed my legs were straight. My trainer came over and could hardly believe his eyes. My deformity was healed!
--Diane Argenzio, Estate Manager, Aspen, Colorado

- 4 -

Transcending a Pattern

TheQuest session with Dr. Ariel was like an exorcism, casting a demon out of my being that was like a leach, sucking the life force out of me, and preventing me from being who I am. After one session, I am a completely different person. I feel differently. My attitude has changed. I definitely have transcended my pattern. I am a whole new being!
--Bruce Travis, Author, Real Estate Broker, Wailea, Hawaii

- 5 -

A Troubled Youth Finds His Way

When meeting with a court-ordered youth, I noticed an enormous shift in his attitude and responsibility in a very short period of time... So I asked him "What has happened to cause you to mature so quickly?" That's when he told me that he was in a program for teens (TheQuest Teen Forum) that was making a huge difference for him.

While he still has a way to go in his life, I have not seen such a huge internal shift in a youth like this in a very long time. My interest in the TheQuest came from seeing results, not from hearing about the program. This is fantastic work! —*Shawn Stevenson, MSW, Youth At Risk Counselor, Case Manager for Youth Zone*

- 6 -
I'm A New Person

After 20 years of being intimately involved in the human potential movement, reading endless material, attending every conference I could, listening to speakers, reading their books, and applying their principles, I was never taken to the places I was told they would take me. They just didn't hold up and I would soon be back into my old patterns without knowing why things were not working for me. Then I met Aurora and started receiving TheQuest sessions.

Right away, after the 1st session, I realized there was a deeper place I needed to go to resolve the issues in my life. I learned the importance of finding the root of the problem instead of adopting a philosophy that sounds great but which doesn't eliminate the effect things have had on my life.

My life has changed considerably with the elimination of stress, eliminating guilt and frustration, and knowing I can be completely honest with myself, and those around me. My self-esteem has been restored to a new high. Each day I look forward to meeting new people, making friends, creating relationships, and enjoying new and exciting experiences. I have a new outlook on life that has never been there before, and I am free to achieve my goals and aspirations. I am so grateful for this life changing experience of TheQuest! --*Bill Mollring, Business Owner*

- 7 -
An Unruly Class Of Teens

I met Dr. Aurora Ariel about two years ago and became interested in her work. I asked if she would be willing to meet with my high school class and give them a 90-minute rendition of what she shares with others in her work with TheQuest.

I have to admit that I was a bit skeptical how this would play out to a group of 20 or so usually somewhat inattentive high school students. She came and met with two of my classes. Both classes were surprisingly attentive and interested in what she presented. All of the students participated, as we were taken through TheQuest, and many shared their process. I also followed along with the class in the exercise she had designed for that day and was amazed at the insights that were provided to me in so brief a period of time.

After the class had ended, several students stayed after class to speak with her further to find out what more they could learn about her work and to thank her for what they had experienced in that short period of time. The fact that she held everyone's attention with something that was somewhat foreign to all of these students and she had all the class thank her as she left for the day and others asking for more, told me that she was on the right track with the work she has dedicated her life to.

I have not met with or seen Aurora in nearly a year since those classes, but I am sure she has accomplished much with her work and will have many good revelations to share with anyone lucky enough to be a part of her teachings or her work. Her method of going inside one's self and healing past issues or gaining self-realizations is really quite amazingly simple, yet very valuable. Like finding a key to a hidden treasure. *--Brad Onsgard, Aspen Police Department, APD-SRO for the Aspen School District*

Appendix

About The Author

Aurora Juliana Ariel, PhD, Creator of TheQuest, and Award Winning Author of the Earth 2012 Series, is a #1 bestselling author, pioneering doctor and healer, whose research and work have given her a profound understanding of the psyche and tools to heal an ailing humanity. She trained under pioneering doctors in alternative medicine, psychology, and holistic health, and holds over 35 certificates and degrees in advanced healing methods as well as a B.A., M.A., and PhD in Psychology.

Dr. Ariel is a Questor Doctor in Total Body Modification, a Certified Zone Therapist and a Certified Practitioner and Instructor of Stress Release Therapies. She is also trained in Edu-Kinesiology, Bio-Kinesiology, Personality Traits and their Relationship to Disease, Immunbiology, Neuro-Emotional Techniques, and more. She has mastered many of the cutting edge counseling techniques of the last century including Gestalt, NLP, Person Centered Counseling, Reality Therapy, Psychosynthesis, Holodynamics, and others. She is also a Kahuna, the successor of Hawaiian Kahuna, Grandmaster Pang.

All of this pales, however, in comparison with the work Dr. Ariel has done on herself and her work directly in the psyche with countless clients over many years. That work has brought forth Dr. Ariel's landmark discoveries, the development of her Counseling Theory and Healing Practice, TheQuest, and TheQuest Self Healing System.

A Spiritual Scientist in the Laboratory of the Soul, Dr. Ariel took her vast body of knowledge and went deeper on her own quest for healing. She discovered a way out of pain and suffering, a transformative technique that changed her life and brought tremendous healing to her clients.

Dr. Ariel has taken TheQuest to the next level and offers it as a complete Self Healing System that includes her powerful seven step Self Counseling technique. Her reason for bringing it to the people, rather than simply releasing it to professional counselors is simple. She wants to bring healing to a world in desperate need.

Dedicated to positive planetary change, Dr. Ariel sees this period on Earth as a time when we, as a humanity, desperately need to uncover and heal the patterning she believes is at the heart of all the dire conditions we are presently facing. When we accomplish this, we become the peaceful, loving, happy individuals we were meant to be and the world changes around us.

For more information about Dr. Ariel, her work, and other products see http://www.AuroraJulianaAriel.com.

To support her efforts, you can make a tax deductible donation to the Institute on her website or at: http://www..IOAH.org or http://www.TheQuest.us.

Your tax deductible donation can be used to donate *TheQuest: Heal Your Life, Change Your Destiny* books or Complete Self Healing System (book, Healing Journal, CD) to rehab centers, prisons, hospitals, health retreats, safe houses for the abused, addiction, abuse, and youth at risk programs, or place of your choice. *Your donations are greatly appreciated!*

TheQuest

TheQuest is a revolutionary breakthrough Counseling Theory and Healing Practice that includes a complete Self Healing System developed by Dr. Ariel after years of extensive research and work. It is designed to bring timely knowledge and a missing piece to rehab centers, prison reform, addiction, youth at risk, 12 step and other programs, greatly increasing their success rate.

For practitioners, it is a way to move your clients quickly from upset to peace, and to help them quickly resolve deep issues, step free of limiting and self sabotaging patterns, addictions, and dysfunctional personality traits, and realize their greater potential.

For the layperson, it is a way to gain greater understanding and mastery of your psychology, empowering authentic self-expression, and creative fulfillment.

For couples, it is an essential ingredient in conscious relationship, where each person works with their own psychology as issues arise. Greater harmony and clear communication can exist when the focus is on resolution through loving, compassionate interactions.

The Institute of Advanced Healing

In 2000, Aurora Juliana Ariel, PhD founded the Institute of Advanced Healing, a non profit organization in Hawaii, to bring forth her life's work, TheQuest, which includes TheQuest Trainings, Classes, Counseling Sessions, Support Groups, advanced healing products and services.

Dr. Ariel developed 7 level certificate training courses, and set up a model chapter in Aspen, Colorado in 2005 to be duplicated around the world by graduates of TheQuest Life Coach and Counselor and Spiritual Leadership Courses.

She has successfully worked with youth at risk, addicts, abusers, and the abused, people with serious illnesses and trauma, and a host of dysfunctional personality traits and life conditions with tremendous results.

She has given classes to teens at High Schools, released TheQuest to the public on her websites, TV, radio, support groups, and via her

Ask Dr. Aurora Column, and is now training people in her seven level Certificate Training Courses provided through the Institute. For more information see http://www.AuroraJulianaAriel.com, http://www.IOAH.org, or http://www.TheQuest.us.

The Human Dilemma

The work at the Institute of Advanced Healing has a very clear focus. To bring TheQuest to a world in dire need. The subconscious programming that has created the human condition with its propensity for misery and suffering must be healed. People worldwide need to understand their psychology and learn how to become masters of their destiny, rather than victims to their fate. The cause of suffering must be healed for the world to begin to reflect the noble ideals that are encoded in the hearts of humanity.

When people are engulfed and entrapped in their human patterns, a higher destiny is never fulfilled. Instead, the destiny that plays out is from this programming. The degree that the higher nature, which Dr. Ariel calls the 'Authentic Self,' can express through the individual, the more the person will be able to experience a higher awareness and ability to attain a greater mastery over their life circumstances. Presently, this is very rare on Earth. Even in the spiritual communities of the world where the greatest trainings and highest information is attained, there is a continual dysfunctional aspect to people's lives, because the subconscious patterns are not being addressed. They are being suppressed or spiritually bypassed, while they continue to work their havoc.

It has long been believed that people cannot change their personality traits or heal their addictions. The best that can be done is for individuals to understand their patterns and strive to overcome them. But this method does not work because physiologically the limbic system, the part of the brain that is activated under stress in what has been called the Fight and Flight Syndrome, is different from the area of the brain where the will and determination is found, which is in the frontal lobe. Therefore, under stress, the individual will revert to Fight and Flight, and the subconscious pattern will begin running. They will move into survival and seek substances or run other addictive behaviors to alleviate suffering. Physiologically, the blood will recede from the frontal lobe impairing will and therefore control.

When the deeper patterns have not been addressed and healed, people will understand their addictions and strive to stay sober or substance free, but if they undergo a series of life stresses, it will be easy for them to fall off the wagon. This is because the subconscious has been left out of the equation.

Currently, because the deeper work is not being done, there is only an 8% success rate in rehab centers and addiction programs. The programs today help strengthen the individual's resolve, but do not provide a complete healing. TheQuest Seven Step Counseling Technique provides the 'missing piece,' which can greatly increase the success rate at these centers and with people suffering from addictions of every kind.

A Breakthrough Technology

Understanding the human dilemma and being concerned that psychologists today normally only scratch the surface when working with clients, thereby keeping people coming for sessions for years without any real movement, Dr. Ariel developed a way to move people quickly through their issues, and heal their underlying patterns. Her revolutionary method provides a complete resolution, healing, and breakthrough in each session.

If you would like to sponsor or support Dr. Ariel's work and the Institute's mission to bring TheQuest to communities throughout the world, donations are tax deductible and greatly appreciated. To make a donation, please go to http://www.AuroraJulianaAriel.com, http://www.IOAH.org, or http://www.TheQuest.us

TheQuest Life Mastery Path

When you understand your psychology, you have greater control over your life circumstances. As you master TheQuest tools and learn how to heal every condition from within, you have a greater command of your destiny. Your Authentic Self is given room for a fuller creative expression in and through you and a new passion and excitement about life returns. You wake up looking forward to each new day and what amazing things will happen next. Unexpected events and synchronistic meetings increase resulting in key alliances with like-minded people for a greater purpose. Life takes on a sweeter quality, as you know you are fulfilling a sacred destiny. TheQuest Life Mastery Path training is available in TheQuest courses, providing you with the tools and knowledge of how to free yourself from every pattern and condition that has limited you, kept you feeling disempowered, burdened, or held back, so that you can realize your full potential.

Heal Your Life, Change Your Destiny

When you heal your life, you change your destiny. It is as if you are defying a powerful law like gravity. For the human patterns within you are creating a different reality than the Life your True Nature would give you. Clearing the way for this Authentic Self to lend its wisdom and power to your life, allows you to fulfill a higher destiny.

TheQuest Life Coach and Counseling Packages

Dr. Ariel has many programs available. (See http://www.AuroraJuliana Ariel.com) These are weekly or bi-monthly sessions (6 months or 1 year) that include Life Coaching and Counseling along with personal training in TheQuest Life Mastery Path. Dr. Ariel is also available at times for personal 7 - 14 day retreats, where her focus is completely on you and your optimum health and well-being, and for Total Life Transformation Intensives (12 weeks) where every area of your life is addressed and transformed.

TheQuest Training

Dr. Ariel is excited to bring TheQuest to your community. If you'd like to sponsor her in your area, receive counseling sessions or life coaching in one of her programs, or receive certification as a Life Coach and Counselor, please email her at: info@aeos.ws.

TheQuest: Heal Your Life, Change Your Destiny Forums consists of three level certificate courses. This training provides an in-depth study of psychology in a format that is experiential, life changing, and empowering.

Each course is unique per the occupants and their current life issues and challenges and is therefore a largely experiential journey to the heart of these conditions where they are healed and transformed. As you learn how to clear a pathway to the Authentic Self and its inner wisdom, you begin to give it more power in your daily life and to live your higher Destiny Potential.

Become a Certified Life Coach and Counselor

TheQuest Life Coach and Counselor 9 month certification course (Level 5) with Dr. Ariel is highly experiential in its application. This program gives you the life mastery skills, knowledge, and tools to become a Life Coach and Counselor, with the ability to practice anywhere in the world.

This course trains you in valuable life mastery skills. Each training provides an in-depth study of psychology and gives you tools to heal self sabotaging patterns, addictions, personality traits, and dysfunctions, deal effectively with health and career issues, and transform challenging relationship dynamics.

In these trainings you learn how to quickly resolve and heal your issues so that you can live more often from your authentic nature. These highly informative trainings are held within a compassionate caring environment and are empowering and life changing.

Accelerated Program for Professionals

Doctors, Psychologists, Health Practitioners, Life Coaches, and Ministers may qualify for the accelerated training program (Level 4) for TheQuest Counselor Certification.

Global Outreach Programs

Dr. Ariel has been developing cutting edge rehabilitation models and programs for prisons, battered women, youth at risk, veterans, and addicts. See more at: http://www.TheQuest.us

A New Frontier in Multimedia Arts

Media is one of the most powerful ways we can facilitate change today because of its immediate affect upon the psyche. Understanding this, Alchemists of the New Millennium know that transmitting positive images, ideas, and language of a beneficial and healing nature can quickly shift consciousness, open up new doorways of thought, and empower individuals to be their best selves.

Through conscious media, we have a tremendous opportunity to assist in this next evolutionary leap in human consciousness and safeguard against the repetition of the mistakes of the past, assisting humanity to become conscious stewards of the earth and inspiring them to bring forth their greatest gifts and achievements on behalf of a people and a planet. By helping catalyze this quantum shift, we become Alchemists of Media who have an important role to play in this New Millennium.

At AEOS, we are determined to make a difference! All our products are exquisitely designed with the highest quality materials, highest vibration of colors, images, and subject matter, and transmit, energetically and creatively, the highest frequencies. We believe our vast array of extraordinary products and services are destined to transform millions of lives throughout the planet.

AEOS, Inc. is a Multimedia Production Company founded by Chairwoman and CEO, Aurora Juliana Ariel, PhD. TheQuest is a proprietary revolutionary breakthrough technology she developed, representing one of the Company's five collections of inspired music, books, and films, placing AEOS on the leading edge in the new psychology/self help genre.

Look for more exciting AEOS products soon, as well as Dr. Ariel's upcoming books in the Earth 2012 series, which delve further into her insights on the worldwide awakening and global renaissance she believes are birthing a New World. To order our products please go to our website at: http://www.AEOS.ws

Healing Inspired Music & Media

Dr. Ariel has studied the powerful influence music and media have on the psyche. She believes that "transformational media is a key to creating the quantum leap in consciousness so necessary at this time, if we are going to avert the many dire potentials before us and positively affect the evolutionary cycle of our planet."

Understanding that conscious media can have a profound and healing influence upon individuals and even transform lives, her greatest love has been to translate her knowledge into multimedia productions that have a healing, uplifting, and inspiring effect. In 2003, she founded AEOS, Inc., a Hawaii based Multimedia Production Company to bring forth her inspired music, books, and films.

In her words, "My joy is in translating the knowledge I have gained into transformational multimedia productions that facilitate positive change within the psyche of humanity, profoundly affecting the consciousness of the planet and assisting humanity to advance forward into an Age of Enlightenment and Peace."

Books & Music CDs by Aurora

Earth 2012: The Ultimate Quest - Vol 1
How To Find Peace In a World of Chaos

Earth 2012: Time of the Awakening Soul - Vol 2
How Millions of People are Changing Our Future

Earth 2012: The Violet Age - Vol 3
A Return to Eden

TheQuest: Heal Your Life, Change Your Destiny
*A Breakthrough Self Healing System*k

Renaissance of Grace
Aurora's World Music CD with Bruce BecVar

Gypsy Soul, Heart of Passion
Gypsy World Music CD by Bruce BecVar & Aurora

River of Gold
New Age Music CD by Bruce BecVar & Aurora

Earth 2012: The Ultimate Quest
How To Find Peace in a World of Chaos

A Life Mastery Path to Unlocking Your Full Potential
By Aurora Juliana Ariel, PhD

AWARD WINNING 1ST BOOK IN EARTH 2012 SERIES
2009 VISIONARY AWARDS

Cataloging the profound shift presently taking place within the psyche of humanity, Dr. Ariel points to the fact that we are living in unprecedented times! Weaving a blend of sacred prophecies, prophetic visions, and scientific predictions around 2012, she unveils a glorious potential that is casting its first rays of light on earth, illuminating the Dark Night we are presently passing through, and providing a "missing piece" to traversing the challenges of this time.

In this first book in the Earth 2012 series, Dr. Ariel guides the reader on a personal quest, providing 7 Master Keys to Inner Peace and a breakthrough Self Counseling Technology, TheQuest, that is easy to apply. Distilled into seven powerful steps, this healing process is designed to accelerate a personal and planetary transformation that could help end suffering on Earth.

Her message, "If we want to avert the dire potentials before us, we must look within and unlock the subconscious patterns behind our challenging life conditions."

Earth 2012: Time of the Awakening Soul
How Millions of People Are Changing Our Future

*A Worldwide Awakening,
Global Renaissance & Glorious Future Unveiled*

By Aurora Juliana Ariel, PhD

The Earth 2012 Saga continues with a Journey into the Miraculous as millions of Awakening Souls alter the course of Earth's Destiny. Weaving a prophetic vision of an Illumined Future, stories of extraordinary encounters reveal the extraordinary time we are in. Find out if you are an Awakening Soul. Take the 22 Master Qualities test.

> "This inspiring, prophetic book speaks to a Soul Awakening that if embraced, can take humanity through a quantum leap into a future Eden that has forever lived as a vision within the hearts of humanity." --John Gray, Author of Men Are From Mars, Women Are From Venus

> "This book rises to the heights of poetry, unveiling a majesty of human potential like a torch in the morning light. It adds its brilliance to what is silently arising all around us."–Jonathan Kolber, Circle of Light

> "A clarion call to consciousness awakening to itself, Earth 2012 quickens spiritual unfolding by lovingly guiding you through one of the most difficult and transformative periods in human history. --Leonard Laskow, M.D., Author of Healing With Love

Earth 2012: The Violet Age
A Return to Eden

Mystical Stories to Inspire the Soul
By Aurora Juliana Ariel, PhD

Miracles abound as the Earth 2012 saga continues. A host of phenomenon behind the Great Awakening are impacting millions of people worldwide. From extraordinary encounters to mystical experiences of every kind, a quantum shift is taking place in the consciousness of humanity.

This book takes us further into the mystical side of our present planetary equation and unveils the mystery behind the Violet People and the unique destiny that drives them to turn the tide at the 11th hour, saving humanity from untold disasters.

While darkness increases on the planet and humanity stands facing gaping jaws of disaster on a Grand Scale, a glorious New World is being birthed from within the psyche of humanity.

"A clarion call to consciousness awakening to itself, the Earth 2012 series quickens spiritual unfolding by lovingly guiding you through one of the most difficult and transformative periods in human history." — Leonard Laskow, M.D., author of Healing With Love

Gypsy Soul, Heart of Passion

Bruce BecVar & Aurora

*Fast paced Nuevo Flamenco Songs
drop into slower, exotic melodies...
As Bruce BecVar's master guitarmanship
weaves a mystical blend of vocals and
gypsy guitar with the transcendent vocals of Aurora
amid violin, pan flutes, and percussion by
a host of illustrious musicians*

Talented musicians grace this gypsy world music album including renowned multi-instrumentalist, Bruce BecVar; Percussionist Rafael Padilla; Peruvian Shaman, Tito La Rosa on Andean Pan Pipes; Gypsy Violinist – Don Lax; Rachel Handlin and Charlie Bisharat on violins, Michael Buono on piano, Steve Reid on percussion, Brandon Fields and Richard Hardy on Saxophone, and Brian BecVar on Synthesizer.

"This album is a therapeutic blend of New Age musical sound graced by the angelic voice of Ariel who is not without her match in BecVar. Ariel and Becvar put together a musical experience worth cherishing. The album's music is relaxingly invigorating and will stimulate you with its deep thought and meaning. An inspiring, earnest and spiritual journey is what you're about to embark on. Think Strunz and Farah on a spiritual path." Manny Auguste, Bryan Farrish Radio Promotion

Aurora's Solo Music CD

Renaissance of Grace

The exotic vocals of Aurora with Bruce BecVar weave a mystical blend that is both uplifting and inspiring, transporting us into a world of transcendence and light.

Talented musicians lend their magic to this gypsy world music album including renowned multi-instrumentalist, Bruce BecVar; Percussionist Rafael Padilla; Peruvian Shaman, Tito La Rosa on Andean Pan Pipes; Gypsy Violinist, Don Lax; Violinist Rachel Handlin, Michael Buono on drums, and Brian BecVar on Synthesizer. Purchase through http://www.AEOS.ws

"Aurora Juliana Ariel is one of those rare artists whose clear voice and beautiful music transmit to more than just the ear, but reaches into the listener's heart with hidden healing messages. Coupled with the extraordinary talent of musician/composer Bruce BecVar, Aurora's offering awakens our inner peace and invites our own calm center to bubble up to the surface. Aurora's mystical language is at once both exotic and familiar, adventurous and comforting. *Renaissance of Grace*, as one of the song titles indicates, is truly a Journey Of The Heart: one pleasurable piece of music after another that you will never want to end. The work as a whole lives up to its name."
-Pamela Polland, *Award Winning Recording Artist, Vocal Coach*

"Journey of the Heart and Shiva Moon are two of the most heartfelt ballads you will hear on any release, their voices soaring together and weaving in and out of fluid guitar lines, gentle piano, bass flute, and percussion. The lyrical romanticism that is expressed owes much to the spirit of Aurora Juliana Ariel, who collaborates with Bruce BecVar to create inspired songs." —DL, *New Age Voice*

River of Gold

Bruce BecVar and Aurora

A brilliant collaboration, River of Gold is a magical weave of guitar, instrumentals, and exotic vocals, this album has been highly acclaimed for the SPECTACULAR LOVE and TRANSCENDENT JOY that fills every note, carrying you into a world of romance, beauty and light.

> *This music uplifts and inspires, enchants and awakens... And keeps you coming back for more!*

Journey of the Heart and Shiva Moon are two of the most heartfelt ballads you will hear on any release, their voices soaring together and weaving in and out of fluid guitar lines, gentle piano, bass, flute, and percussion. The lyrical romanticism that is expressed owes much to the spirit of Aurora Juliana Ariel, who collaborates with Bruce BecVar to create inspired songs ... ~ DL, New Age Voice

The sweet duet "Journey of the Heart" is a dance of masculine and feminine voices delicately interspersed with exqusite guitar rhythms. As I listen to this and other pieces, I am transported to a land where love and romance abound and the beauty of nature flows through my heart like a river of gold. This recording is deeply passionate, exotic, and simply unforgettable. ~ Betty Timm

BecVar generates electricity in partnership with vocalist and co-producer Aurora. Abundantly intimate, this album is nothing less than a magnificent mash note, a Valentine that all can share. –PJ Birosik

Order Now at http://www.AuroraMusic.ws